Strike It Rich With Pocket Change

by Brian Allen and Ken Potter

No Experience Needed!

Published by

An Imprint of F+W Publications

700 East State Street • Iola, WI 54990-0001
715-445-2214 • 888-457-2873

Our toll-free number to place an order or obtain
a free catalog is (800) 258-0929.

Library of Congress Catalog Number: 2006933682

ISBN 13-digit: 978-0-89689-442-6
ISBN 10-digit: 0-89689-442-8

Designed by Stacy Bloch and Wendy Wendt
Edited by Randy Thern

Printed in the United States of America

HOW TO USE THIS BOOK

1. Read every page of this book completely and study areas pointed out in photos with arrows.

2. Have coins suspected to be varieties verified by one or more of the professional attributers listed in the last chapter of this book.

3. Market your finds via one of the methods described in Chapter 10.

4. Cash your checks and have fun.

5. Repeat steps 1-4 for more fun and profit.

Updated prices for coins listed in this book can be found on our web-site: http://koinpro.tripod.com/Treasures.htm

AUTHOR'S DISCLAIMER

The prices listed within this book are believed by the authors to be an accurate reflection of current retail prices at the time of publication. Use these prices as a guide only and not an absolute. Market values may change up or down depending on supply and demand and other market conditions.

The descriptions and analysis given within this book are those of the authors. Every effort has been made to provide the most accurate information possible. The authors may not be held responsible to any errors found within this book.

DEDICATIONS

From Brian:

I dedicate my efforts to the memories and efforts of three very close friends and fellow warriors; they have paid the ultimate sacrifice while heroically serving in the Armed Forces; Chief Warrant Officer Stanley Harriman, Sergeant First Class Peter Tycz, and Sergeant First Class Christopher Speer.

I am forever grateful to have served with such remarkable men and that I was somehow worthy of their friendship. Rest in Peace.

From Ken:

From the very beginning of my involvement in this great hobby, my brother Don was at my side. In the early 1960s, we spent hours together at Metropolitan Savings and Loan on the corner of Seven Mile and Evergreen in Detroit, searching through Lincoln cent rolls for early dates, anything with an "S" Mint mark, "steel cents," and the occasional error. As we got older we rode bikes to Livonia Mall and attended the local coin show and auction. We collected coins from our pre-teen years all the way into our adulthood, sharing our knowledge and exchanging ideas on things like which coins would go up in value the fastest or which were the most beautiful designs. We visited numerous shops and admired each others purchases or finds.

Our first real major discovery of a variety was together when in response to a Coin World article we checked Don's box of five Canadian 1973 proof-like sets for the newly discovered "Large Bust" quarters of which we were lucky enough to find two.

Later we developed a devotion to the sport of fishing and purchased a boat and motor and spent many hours together developing our skills on every lake, river, pond, and stream we could find.

Don died of a heart attack at the age of 47 on December 3, 1999. He was my best friend and will be sorely missed. I dedicate this book to his memory.

TABLE OF CONTENTS

INTRODUCTION

Why Search Your Pocket Change?

Have you ever knowingly spent $100 on a candy bar or $50 on a soft-drink? As ludicrous as the concept sounds, there is no doubt that you have unintentionally done this numerous times without ever knowing it. The fact is, billions of coins pass through the public's hands every day and of these coins, a small but significant percentage contain variations in design or errors that make them different than the rest. Many of these varieties are the target of avid collectors who are often willing to pay significant premiums to acquire them. Searching your pocket change can be fun and profitable! It can be done alone or as a leisurely pastime with the entire family.

In many ways, searching your pocket change for hidden treasures is like accepting lotto tickets in lieu of your change at the local grocer – except that you can never really "lose" by checking your change. You certainly wouldn't accept lotto tickets without scrutinizing them to see if you're a winner – so why bypass the possibility of a quick windfall by failing to search your pocket change?

The next Lincoln cent you look at could be worth $50,000! Just two examples of error Lincoln cents that could be lurking in your pocket change right now are the 1969-S and the 1970-S "Doubled Dies." Both coins were struck from imperfectly prepared dies resulting in a strongly doubled date and lettering on all the coins produced from those individual dies. Because tens-of-thousands of dies are required to produce our nation's coinage for just one year and because errant dies are often detected and removed from service early, it can be extremely difficult to locate any of the coins produced from an imperfect die. Both of the coins mentioned above appear to be from dies whose flaws were detected early resulting in very short runs.

While we freely acknowledge that you may never find a coin worth this much, it is a fact that thousands of other coins are circulating that are worth anywhere from $5 to $500 or more and that are easier to find than you might at first think. Finding them just takes a bit of knowledge as to where to look and a few basic tools.

Coin Collecting (known as "numismatics") is one of the oldest hobbies known to man. In the early days it was considered the "hobby of the rich," and even rulers of ancient kingdoms are known to have collected coins. However, the collecting of Mint errors and varieties is a relatively new dimension of numismatics that has firmly established itself within the hobby in the last several decades. The U.S. Mint's new 50 States quarter program, the introduction of a new dollar coin, and recent media attention to several "rare errors" has spurred a welcomed increase in public awareness of what can be found in circulating coinage, although much of it has also led to misconceptions as to what is collectable and valuable and what is not.

The purpose of this book is to dispel the myths and assist you in discovering, marketing, and researching rare coins that you can find in your pocket change. While its focus is on the more valuable items that can be found, readers should be aware that thousands of other less valuable varieties and errors (that fall into the $2 to $10 range) can be found in pocket change, and that many others of great rarity and value can be found on older, obsolete coinage generally found by searching dealer's stocks at coin shops or shows. If we have whet your appetite sufficiently to have stirred an interest in the "lesser items" or the obsolete coinage, we encourage you to investigate some of the more specialized publications that are listed in Chapter 9 of this book.

ACKNOWLEDGMENTS

This book would not have been possible without the aid of the many collectors, dealers, and researchers who contributed to the project. The information provided by these persons and institutions assisted in numerous ways ranging from variety selection (what was appropriate for the book), pricing, photography and layout. We would like to give special thanks and recognition to the persons and institutions listed below for making this publication an enjoyable and worthy project. The authors apologize to anyone who provided assistance but whose name was inadvertently left off of this list. To all those who made this book come together, Thank You!

Abbott's Corporation
ANACS
Eric Axtell
Frank Baumann
Peter Bean
John Bordner
Larry Briggs
Gary Burger
Mike Byers
Jennifer Cassanza
L&C Coin
CoinWorld
Curtis Colin
Larry Comer
CONECA
Billy G. Crawford
Cumberland Coins & Cards
Mike Decarter
Mike Diamond
Gene Dorrough

Mike Ellis
Mike Fahey
Bill Fivaz
Kevin Flynn
Ft. Bragg Federal Credit Union
Pete Goydos
James Green
Lloyd Hanson
Alan Herbert
Heritage Coin
Gary Kelly
H.M. Kuykendall
GJ Lawson
Russ LeBeau
Lonesome John Devine
Mark Longas
Sam Lukes
Arnie Margolis
John Martin

John Mellyn
BJ Neff
Erik Nielson
NCADD
NGC
Neil Osina
Ron Pope
Brian Ribar
Jimi Ribar
Bill and Debbie Rourke
Pamala Ryman
SEGS
Mickey Smith
JT Stanton
Tonja Stump
Fred Weinberg
John A. Wexler
John Wills Rare Coins
Tim Wissert

We would like to give special thanks to John Bordner, Billy G. Crawford, Mike Diamond, Kevin Flynn, Numismatic Guarantee Corporation (NGC), J.T. Stanton, Fred Weinberg, and John Wexler for supplying and granting permission to use a number of the photos appearing in this book.

The authors of this book owe a very special thanks to Melissa Justice for her invaluable editing. Her attention to detail is represented throughout this book.

AGE DOES NOT ALWAYS EQUATE VALUE

A common myth held by non-collectors is that the older the coin the more valuable it is. Nothing could be further from the truth. While many coins increase in value with age, supply and demand are the most significant factors related to their increase in value. (The metal content of a coin is, of course, another obvious factor contributing to value. It stands to reason that a gold coin is often more valuable than one comprised of copper just based on its gold value alone.)

To illustrate, many Morgan silver dollars from the 19th century are worth less than $10 while a 1996-W U.S. Silver Eagle dollar coin has a current value exceeding $2000.00. The difference in values between these two coins is astounding to the new collector but is a perfect example of a priced based on supply and demand. In the case of many Morgan dollars, they were minted in the millions and barely circulated since consumer demand for them at the time of minting was low. As a result, many still existed in uncirculated to almost uncirculated grades in the Treasury's vaults way up into the 1960s when the supply finally ran dry. Today, most Morgan dollar dates are in such plentiful supply that even though the coin is in high demand by collectors, many dates can be had in uncirculated grades for under $50.00. On the contrary, the 1996-W Silver Eagle dollar was only minted for inclusion in a set

1906 Indian Cent $1.30-$2.50

Good to Very Fine condition

1929 Buffalo Nickel .60c-$1.75

Good to Very Fine condition

containing the 1996-W Gold Eagle series (Including a 1/10th, 1/4, 1/2 and 1 oz piece), in very limited supply. Demand from Silver Eagle collectors needing this specially produced coin boasting the West Point Mint Mark quickly outstripped supply and the price skyrocketed.

Another good example of age not contributing significantly to the value of a coin can be drawn from a look at ancient coin values. While some are quite valuable, you can find offerings of "common" ancient coins from 2000 years ago at prices ranging from $7-$30.

Other coins often saved with the belief they are valuable because they are no longer being produced but are actually of little demand can be found described in the back of the book under "MYTHS."

The best way to educate yourself on coin values is to purchase a price guide from your local coin dealer or bookstore or to subscribe to one of the many coin periodicals. These types of books and magazines are not expensive and are very easy to understand.

CIRCULATED COIN CONDITIONS

Unless a coin has come straight out of a fresh roll and into your hand, the vast majority of coins you will encounter in everyday commerce will be circulated coins that will show varying degrees of wear. These coins are evaluated by "grades" ranging from "Almost Good" to "About Un-circulated." These verbal designations are used as a form of shorthand to describe the amount of wear on a coin. The less wear a coin shows, the more it is worth for that date and type. It is very important to learn how to grade since the value of a coin can vary greatly depending on this factor. A coin at the lower end of the grading spectrum valued at $5 could be worth $500 at the upper end.

There are several moderately priced books that fully illustrate and describe the characteristics of each grade. These books may be obtained through coin shops or book stores. You may also be able to obtain them through your local library.

The following are general standards for circulated coins that you may encounter (consult a grading guide for the specifics relating to each coin type):

About Good (AG) - Very heavily worn with portions of the lettering, devices or date missing or barely visible. The date must always be legible or it will grade "Poor" to "Fair," (two grades that we will not cover here as you should never encounter them in circulation). AG (and lower) grades are generally associated with obsolete coinage types from eras bygone when coins were less inclined to be removed from circulation by collectors or be melted by the government due to damage or wear. These obsolete types were the backbone of commerce, much like our $1 through $20 bills are today and spent virtually no time locked up in piggy banks or shoved into desk drawers (save for during times of financial crisis or hoarding). Thus, they circulated more extensively for far longer periods of time than their modern counterparts. Today, an AG (or lower grade) coin in circulation is a rarity.

Good (G) - Heavily worn, all major details of the coin are visible, but may be faint in some areas. All lettering must be separate from the rims. Raised areas on the coin must be slightly raised although the detail may be absent. The coin rims should be raised.

Very Good (VG) - Well worn, all major details of the coin are visible, but may be faint in some areas. Raised areas on the coin must be fully raised and the details must be visible. The coin rims should be fully raised.

Fine (F) - Moderate wear, the central design is bold, all lettering is well defined with slight weakness permitted.

Very Fine (F) - Light wear on the surface, all details and lettering are bold, and only the high points of the coins features show light wear.

Extra Fine (EF or XF) - Light overall wear on the coin's high points, all details are very sharp, and may contain traces of mint luster in the protected areas of the coin.

About Uncirculated (AU)- Very slight traces of wear may be seen on the highest point on the coin's obverse and reverse. These coins will often have mint luster and may look uncirculated with the exception of wear on the high points of the coin. They may range from red to brown in coloration for copper and white to almost black for silver.

UNCIRCULATED COIN CONDITIONS

There are 11 different grades used to describe uncirculated coins. Differentiation of these grades requires the trained eye of a well seasoned collector or dealer. Some coins are unknown in uncirculated condition or in the upper levels of the uncirculated range. This contributes significantly to the value of some coins. Fortunately, one point difference between the grades of most coins falling in the lower half of the uncirculated range often make little differences in a coin's value. However, if your coin appears to fall in the upper levels of the uncirculated grades and is a candidate for carrying a hefty price tag, it is best to consult with a professional or have the coins graded and encapsulated by a grading company.

Grading uncirculated coins takes dedication and experience but is well worth the time to learn if you intend to grade coins for yourself. Do not be afraid to visit shops and coin shows to study coins that have been graded by professional grading services or to consult with a knowledgeable dealer. Most importantly, arm yourself with the proper books and study them over and over. Start with our recommended book list and check your local library.

*OFFICIAL A.N.A GRADING STANDARDS FOR UNITED STATES COINS (c) American Numismatic Association ISBN: 0-307-19876-6

*PHOTOGRADE, *Official Photographic Grading Guide For United States Coins.* By James F. Ruddy ISBN: 0-307-99361-2 (For circulated conditions only)

*A large selection of other suggested books is listed in Chapter 11 of this book.

FOR YOUR INFORMATION...........

This type of Minor Error is called a "misaligned die." The error will show one side of the coin that is slightly off-center with the opposite side centered correctly. This is a common error and is normally sold for $2-$5. To be of value, the off-center side must be missing at least one side of the coin's rim. The one shown here is very minor and of little value.

TOOLS OF THE TRADE

Your eyes and a good basic text book on error coins are all that is necessary for you to get started in recognizing major errors types like Off Metals, Off Centers and Clips (see Chapter 8). However, these are most often quickly found by counting room operations and rarely filter down to the man-on-the-street. Most of the errors and varieties that are out there hiding in your pocket change, and which are the main focus of this book, are microscopic in nature. They will require some magnification.

There are a few basic tools necessary for you to begin your search for these types of errors and varieties. Naturally, you need this book (and/or other authoritative references) that provide detailed information, complete with high quality photographs. Authoritative reference material will allow you to ascertain whether or not what you have found is a collectable type. Additionally, you will need a good high-quality magnifying glass and a maneuverable light source.

CORRECT

This is the proper method to examine coins with a magnifying glass. Notice the distance between the glass and the coin in relation to the eye. Notice the position of the light allowing for maximum reflection off of the coin surface.

INCORRECT

This is the improper method of using a magnifying glass.

Magnifying Glasses

There are thousands of minor varieties of lesser prominence than those listed in this book that may require magnifications of 14-Power (14x) to 20x. These offer profit potential and you have to decide if you want to invest in the magnifiers required to find them or restrict your search to the big-ticket items. For the record, 5x-7x magnification is generally accepted as best for grading coins, and 10x to 14x for attributing a variety. The authors prefer to own a WW, 10x, 14x and 20x in addition to a microscope with a range of

10x-60x. We use 5x-7x for grading, and 10x for quick scans of coins at coin shows (when time is of the essence and we are restricting our search to the more major varieties). A 10x glass is easier on the eyes and has a wider field of view than the stronger glasses – it will allow you to look at more coins faster. A 14x glass is used for a closer look at a variety that has already been identified or double checking pieces that we think may show something we missed with a 10x glass. A 14x glass may replace a 10x glass altogether, but it is harder on the eyes and you will tire more quickly than with a 10x. A 20x glass does the same thing that the 14x did for the 10x and may be used to confirm that an item is actually a triple Mint mark rather than a double Mint mark, etc. A 20x has a tiny field of view and is extremely hard on the eyes. If you decide to buy one, it will rarely find use, but there will be times you find it handy.

No, you do not need all these magnifiers to get started, but you will probably want to at least have a 5x for grading at a cost of about $8 and a 10x Hastings Triplet at about $19.95, for the economy models made by Anco (the same lens by Bausch & Lomb will cost you about double that figure but is lighter and of far superior construction).

Do not buy one of the standard 16x styles (these we c all "metal monsters") as these are not of the Hastings Triplet design and carry significant distortion undesirable to searching for varieties. In addition, contrary to the implication that they are of about 16 power, they are actually only about 10x.

Lighting

Any type of lighting will sufficiently assist you with examining your coins; however, you must have the light source close to you and the coin. The goose-neck style lamp that can be fixed to the side of a desk with a clamp is best due to its stability and maneuverability but basic desk lamps with soft-white light bulbs are very affordable and more than likely already in your home and will be sufficient to get you started. You may even use a typical living room lamp with a 75 watt light bulb by angling the lamp shade to direct light toward your position. The proper lighting, regardless of the source, will allow you the ability to rotate or angle your coin to capture the light and locate that rare error in your pocket change!

**Off-Center 25c
$7-$10 Value**

PRESERVING YOUR FINDS

One of the most important aspects in maintaining a coin's "grade" is preservation. There are a number of different commercially marketed holders that are very inexpensive and recommended for coin storage. The most popular of these holders are referred to as "2x2's" (named after the actual size of the holder). For a large number of coins, you can purchase "tubes"— a plastic holder that will hold a roll of a particular denomination. These holders not only provide protection but also provide a place to label your find and ensure that it is not lost or slipped back in with other coins. Coin holders can be obtained from coin dealers, and some book stores and department stores that carry hobby supplies. They are also easily obtained from mail order dealers found advertising in coin publications.

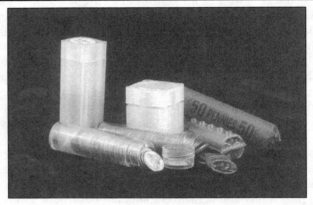

"Tubes" are commonly used to store a number of coins. These can be purchased from most coin dealers. These tubes are very inexpensive and worth the minimal cost to ensure that your finds do not slip back into circulation due to error.

For single coins, 2x2's (sometimes referred to as "flips") are the preferred method of storage. These can be purchased at large retail stores, book stores, and local coin dealers.

For cheap and quick storage you can use empty film tubes and envelopes. Be sure to write the contents on the outside for easy identification.

Professional Coin Grading and Encapsulation

Another method of preservation is the encapsulation of rare coins by professional grading services. This practice is commonly referred to as "slabbing" because the large plastic holders used to encapsulate the coins resemble a "slab." These services offer to grade, attribute, and preserve your coins in those tamper-resistant plastic holders for a fee that depends on the speed and type of service you desire. The encapsulation of your coins will not only preserve their condition, but they will also assist you with selling to perspective buyers who may place a greater trust in the impartial grade assigned by the grading service than that of the seller.

CLEANING COINS

Never clean a coin! Regardless of the debris, darkness, or current surface condition of a coin, it should never be cleaned. Any form of rubbing, dipping, or cleaning of a coin can cause further damage to the surface and decrease its value. Most dealers or collectors do not invest in cleaned coins and would rather leave the coin in the natural circulated state. If the amount of damage is to the extent that a particular variety is difficult to view, you will have trouble liquidating the coin to perspective buyers anyway — cleaning will only complicate matters.

Valuable Forms of Doubling
VS
Other Forms of Doubling

Many collectors interested in valuable "doubled dies" and "repunched mint marks" (RPMs), have trouble distinguishing them from other forms of doubling. This includes several forms not considered particularly collectable or valuable. Many are "mechanical" in nature and originate during the striking or ejection of the coin from the press, while others are the result of die deterioration. While the collectable forms of "die doubling" are created due to misalignments of multiple images being impressed into a die, the less desirable forms of doubling actually have their origins in the erosion or alteration of existing design and really have nothing to do with distinct die variety or an errant die being produced. The descriptions and images below should aid in your understanding of these differences.

Doubled Dies
(Extremely Collectable)

Hub doubled dies (commonly referred to simply as "doubled dies") are the result of the multiple hubbing process. A hub is a master tool made in hardened steel that contains an exact image of a coin. It is used to impress its design into working dies that are then used to strike coins. Hub doubling is possible on many world coins due to a phenomenon known as work hardening (which causes the metal of the face of a die to become too hard and brittle to allow a complete image to be sunk into a die in one operation). Several impressions or hubbings are required to produce a die using the multiple hubbing process. (In recent years, the multiple hubbing process has been replaced by several world Mints, including the United States Mint, by the more modern "single squeeze" *restrained hubbing* process which virtually eliminated the possibility of hub doubling on coins in the United States starting in 1997 for the cent and five cent coins and the balance of denominations in 1998).

Between each hubbing, the die is removed from the press and annealed (softened) thus allowing for another impression without shattering the die. This process is repeated until a satisfactory image is achieved. If a misalignment of images occurs due to improper indexing during the reinstallation of a partially finished die into a hubbing press for a subsequent impression, a doubled die results.

Most forms of hub doubling show as well-rounded overlapping images in relief, with distinct separation lines between those images. You can actually tool.

Doubled dies have proven extremely popular with collectors and often command very significant premiums over the normal value of the coin.

Repunched Mint Marks
(Extremely Collectable)

Up until 1990, all Mint marks were punched into otherwise completed regular coinage dies individually with a hand punch and mallet. This process allowed for variations in the placement of the Mint mark, variations in its strength and sometimes whether it went into the die at a angle or perfectly flush with the field or titled clockwise or counterclockwise. It often required several taps of the mallet to sufficiently sink the Mint mark into a die. At times, a punch appears to have been angled too far in one direction creating weakness at one side and strength at the other. This was compensated for with a correction that angled later taps of the punch in the direction of weakness. Other times, the engraver probably examined his work and decided it needed strengthening and thus setting the punch back down for another blow. Still other times, a first impression of a Mint mark was up way too high encroaching into the date, or far too low, or perhaps even rotated at an unacceptable angle that could be as severe as 180 degrees (resulting in an inverted Mint mark)! These factors and plain old-fashioned "punch bounce" are all conditions that are known to have caused RPMs.

The diagnostics of RPMs, (and other forms of repunching not covered in this book), are identical to that of Doubled Dies; there will be separation lines between overlapping images and lots of total separation in the form of "split serifs."

Strike Doubling
(Non-collectable)

Most often doubled dies and RPMs will show as overlapping images that are rounded and in relief with some degree of separation between images; "Strike Doubling" appears as a shelf-like extension next to the affected design(s). This effect is illustrated on the date and Mint mark of the 1969-S Lincoln cent shown on the next page. This form of "strike doubling" is the result of "die bounce" that may occur within a split second after the strike. Note that there is no separation of design and that the original raised portions of the date and the Mint mark have been smashed or pushed into the field resulting in the flat shelf-like appearance. On uncirculated coins, the shelf often has a shiny appearance identical to what you'd see on a fresh scrape. This is because the original Mint luster was destroyed by the scraping of the die on the design when the shelf was created. Compare this coin to the genuine 1969-S doubled die cent on page 42.

"Strike Doubling" is often referred to by others as: "machine doubling damage," "mechanical doubling," "chatter," "die bounce," and a host of other terms. They all refer to the same basic type of doubling. It is very common on many dates of U.S. coins and is not considered particularly collectable by most specialists. We assign no extra value to this type and consider it a form of damage on the coin because it occurs after the coin was struck.

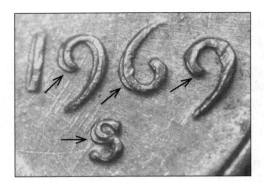

Strike doubling shown
on the date of the
1969-S Lincoln Cent

The 1971 doubled die cent shown below is a superb example of "hub doubling" or what is commonly referred to as a "doubled die." Notice that you are looking at overlapping images with some areas of the word LIBERTY showing total separation between individual letters. The doubling is well rounded and exhibits Mint luster on both the primary and secondary images.

Here is another example of strike doubling on a 1968-S Lincoln cent. Notice that there is no separation of design and that the secondary image is flat and shelf-like in appearance. Also note, that unlike doubled dies, the remnants of what is left of the original raised undisturbed portions of the date are now narrower than normal since parts of it have been flattened down into the shelf.

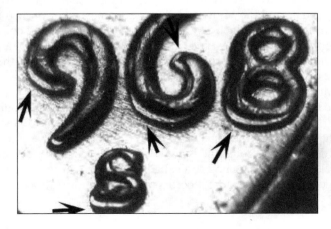

Flat Field Strike Doubling
(Low Interest Collectable)

Another form of "strike doubling" that occurs on coins is what we refer to as "Flat Field Strike Doubling" (FFSD). The most frequent cause occurs when the upper, "hammer die," slams down on a coinage blank (known as a planchet) and imparts a light partial image on the planchet a split second before the ram bottoms out and applies the pressure required to form the complete image on the coin. If there is any "slop" in the press in the form of loose die bolts, etc., then a slight slippage can occur between the first impact of the die with the planchet and the impact of the ram exerting the primary force necessary to strike the coin. This may cause doubling of some or all the images on the coin. It is characterized by a shelf of doubling that · is clearly outlined but struck flat with the field of the coin. Since these minor images caused by the initial kiss of the die are essentially "restruck" by the dies, when the pressure is applied by the ram, they will show Mint luster and have no effect on the primary image that can be of normal diameter.

However, due to the slop in the press, "Flat Field Doubling" is often found in combination with the more common form of strike doubling described previously. Shown is a look at LIB of LIBERTY found on a 1970-S Lincoln cent which displays a good example of FFSD.

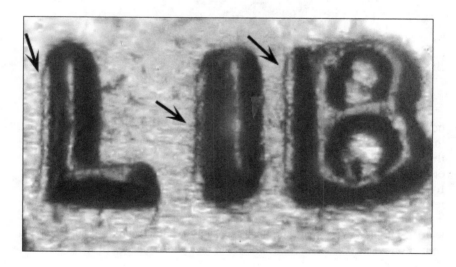

Since FFSD occurs within the Minting process, it technically is a legitimate Mint error. However, few collectors or even researchers understand it, and it is often mis-diagnosed as regular "strike doubling" and assessed as a "damaged coin" rather than an error. Few collectors have expressed an interest in this error type and as such we assign no extra value to it except for the most extreme examples on proof coins.

Ejection Doubling
(Non-collectable)

Another form of strike doubling that occurs to coins is known as "Ejection Doubling." It occurs when a coin sticks to a lower die and is virtually ripped off the die during its ejection from the press by the feeder/ejector fingers or other ejection systems. The doubling will show as a raised knife-like burr on the effected design elements. Here we show the reverse of a 1959 Lincoln cent showing "Ejection Doubling" on the lettering of STATES OF and E PLURIBUS UNUM.

Because this form of doubling occurs after the coin is struck, it is considered a form of damage to which we assign no extra value.

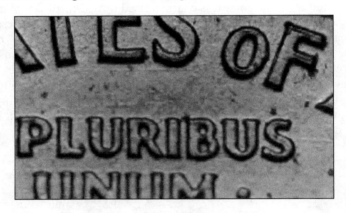

Die Deterioration Doubling
(Very Low Interest)

Another very common form of doubling found on coins is "Die Deterioration Doubling," (DDD). It is the result of die wear or improper heat treating (of the dies) combined with die wear. The effects manifest themselves as doubling, thickening, twisting and other deformities usually most pronounced on lettering or other designs closest to the rim and progressing inward on extreme examples. It is often found in combination with heavy die flow lines or irregular fields often referred to as the "orange peel fields." DDD takes on a variety of looks depending on the geometry of the design, metals being struck, pressures used, and other factors. This makes it difficult to illustrate exactly what it might look like on every coin. However, we show several examples to give you some idea of it's general characteristics.

Bear in mind that DDD is most common during years of high coinage output when the Mints are forced to extend the use of dies to their extreme limits. Although DDD can be found on almost any date, it is very common on the "steel cents" of 1943 (where it can be extremely pronounced) on other Lincoln cents starting in the 1950s and on Jefferson nickels and Washington quarters, thus becoming almost epidemic on the nickels since the early 1960s and on the quarters starting in 1965. The other denominations not mentioned seem to be affected a bit less due to less demand to strike them or to fewer encounters.

Due to world record coinage output of the State commemorative quarters, DDD has been exceedingly common on these issues and is expected to continue to be so.

 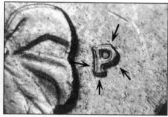

Shown above are examples of DDD on the obverse of a 1993-P Washington Quarter (on the P Mint Mark and on IN GOD WE TRUST) and on the reverse lettering of a 1983-D Jefferson nickel.

DDD is a legitimate die variation but is inherently dynamic, so much so that it is impossible to catalog it by stages. It is also considered by most as a "normal" part of die-use and nothing out of the ordinary. For these reasons and because it is extremely common — nobody catalogs it and very few knowledgeable die variety specialists bother to collect it. We assign no extra value to this form of doubling on U.S. coins.

In contrast, we show a hub doubled die on IN GOD WE TRUST on a 1946 Roosevelt dime. Compare this doubling to the doubling on the 1993-P Washington quarter shown previously. Notice the overlap of images and strong separation lines on the doubled die.

Plating Split Doubling
(Non-collectable)

Lincoln cents struck since mid-1982 are comprised of a thin layer of copper plating bonded to a solid core of zinc. This plating can be stretched so thin during the striking of a coin that it may fracture around the boundaries of certain designs — in particular those that are at a sharp angle to the field like the Mint mark. When such fractures occur, not only do they expose a narrow band of zinc but a thin section of plating often snaps back and creates a ridge-like pile-up that is slightly raised and can look similar to the remnant of a weak Denver Mint mark (when it occurs next to the "D"). It may also occur around other designs, (such as IN GOD WE TRUST), but is often less pronounced since the balance of designs are hubbed into the die and are usually more rounded to the field.

Plating Split Doubling is a very minor defect and inherent to the process. We add no extra value to this variation.

Shown below are three different Mint marks exhibiting Plating Split Doubling.

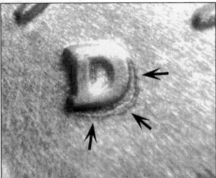

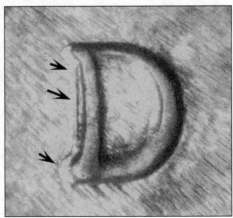

Plating Blisters
(Non-collectable)

Plating blisters may occur in isolated areas or all over the surfaces of a copper plated zinc cent. The blisters are most often the result of condition known as "foaming," associated with the use of contaminated electrolyte and used to facilitate the electroplating of the cent blanks. Other organic pollutants affecting the plating or zinc oxidation may also be factors.

These blisters take on numerous shapes and sizes and when shaped "just right" and located next to a Mint mark, may be confused with an RPM.

Shown is a photo of a 1982-D with a plating blister mimicking an RPM. Plating blisters, though often tolerated by collectors, are considered less than desirable and we assign no extra value to them.

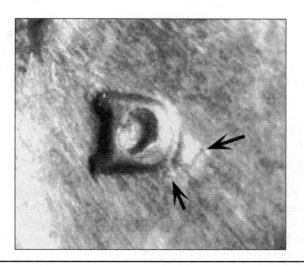

Broadstruck Lincoln Cent with Indent. $15-$30 Value

A "filled" or "clogged" Lincoln Cent. .50¢ -$3 Value

Treatment of Minor Varieties and Errors

When you first start examining coins with a magnifying glass it will open up a word filled with what appears to be irregularities that you will think, "just have to be valuable errors and varieties!" At first you may feel it's "beginner's luck" and you've magically struck a gold mine! Valuable coins that nobody before you seemed lucky enough to encounter, are yours for the taking! Almost every handful of coins you check turns up significant numbers of "valuable" errors! You start to envision trips to the Virgin Islands or a new boat docked out in front of your new condo on the lake. Some of these "errors" may in fact be legitimate but others will be imagined – like angels in the clouds. Still others will represent little more than reflections or shadows that you just haven't become accustomed to recognizing.

At about the point you've stacked up your first fortune – it's time for a reality check. The fact is, valuable error coins are not found in circulation in short periods of time in quantities measured in stacks. It's a lot like fishing. The first few times out you may catch a lot of snags and/or wander over to a "nursery area" and catch a bunch of small fry! Generally speaking – the big fish just aren't going to jump into the boat and it's going to take a bit of time, practice, and experience to start consistently catching the big ones.

In the beginning, you are most likely to find large numbers of minor variations such as die cracks, die chips, die scratches, plating blisters, die flow lines, missing or weak design elements due to die abrasion, die deterioration doubling, double rims, and minor clash marks. These are very common on most issues of world coins and are not necessarily anything out of the ordinary.

Traditionally, these types of variations hold very little monetary value over face value. Yes, a collector or dealer may run an ad and sell a few at an inflated price to unknowledgeable collectors, but the fact is there is not a single dealer involved in the error-variety hobby that will purchase such items for resale, and few (if any) of today's sellers will be willing buyers of these items tomorrow. Are these varieties interesting? Yes! And they are very collectable too! They are also of extremely high educational value. The area of die chips, cracks, etc., is where many of the old-time-error-variety collectors started out ... and there is a lot to be learned about dies and the minting process by studying such items. Valuable? Well - if I can't find an error-variety dealer that will buy them, much less handle them - then I must conclude they are of little value over face. We suggest you have fun searching and keep as many as you like as long as you're not paying over face value. Just realize you're collecting them for fun and education and that no resale market to dealers exists.

It should be noted that there is always an exception to the rule! Exceptions include coins like the 1922 No D cent, the 1937-D 3 Legged Buffalo nickel and the 1982 "No FG" Kennedy halves. All exhibit very trivial flaws of a class normally ignored by collectors that have been promoted into high demand "major errors."

While 99.9% of the "minors" are ignored by the majority of collectors and dealers, you just never know which will be the next to catch on. It probably wouldn't hurt to hold on to a few of the more interesting ones to see what happens.

"BIE Cents"

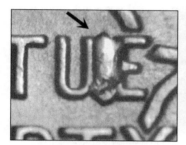

States Quarters with interesting die breaks

Clashed Die
"Prisoner Cent"

While the vast majority of minor errors described in this chapter carry no premium, a few do carry modest premiums of 50c to $5. Lincoln Cents with a die break between the BIE of LIBERTY (referred to as "BIE CENTS"), interesting die breaks on States Quarters, and Clashed Dies are a few examples of minor varieties which carry a value.

HOW TO USE THIS BOOK

BEST LOCATION
TO VISUALIZE
THE VARIETY

BRIEF DESCRIPTION OF
WHAT TO LOOK FOR

DATE AND VARIETY

1960-D Large Date   Doubled Mint Mark

FAIR
MARKET
VALUE

Look at: The D below the date
Look for: A very bold and wide second D to the left.

PHOTO OF
WHERE TO
LOOK ON
THE COIN

VALUE:

Extra Fine		About Uncirculated	Uncirculated
2.00	2.75		12.00

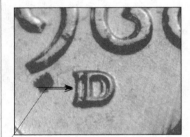

Listing Numbers
CONECA: RPM-001
Potter:VCR#4/RPM#2
Wexler: WRPM-001

Area of
Error

Listing Numbers
Breen#2237
CONECA: RPM-001
Potter:VCR#1/RPM#1
Wexler: WRPM-001

Listing Numbers are the numbers assigned by individual attributers. Not all attributers agree on each and every variety, therefore some coins may not be listed by all attributers. You will want to use these numbers when advertising your coin. For a more detailed explanation of each attributer's origin view the Coin Terms in the back of this book.

Strike It Rich With Pocket Change

LINCOLN CENT VARIETIES

Composition: Copper 0.950 - Tin and Zinc 0.05
Years: 1959-1962
Weight: 3.11 Grams
Diameter: 19mm

Composition: Copper 0.950 and Zinc 0.05
Years: 1963-1982
Weight: 3.11 Grams
Diameter: 19mm

Composition: 97.5% Zinc Core with 2.5% Copper Plating
Years: 1982-Present
Weight: 2.5 Grams
Diameter: 19 mm

Years of Mint Marks
Philadelphia 1959-Present
Denver 1959D-1964D, 68D-Present
San Francisco 1968S-1974S

Look at: D Mint mark below the date
Look for: Remnants of a 2nd and 3rd Mint mark are visibly protruding from under the primary "D" to the west and south (see arrows).

VALUE:

Extra Fine	About Uncirculated	Uncirculated
1.00	2.75	15.00

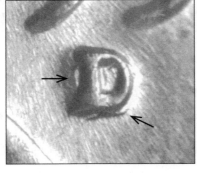

Listing Numbers
Cherrypickers': FS-022.5
CONECA: RPM-001
Potter:VCR#1/RPM#1
Wexler: WRPM-001

1959-D

Possible "D" in Date

Look at: The second 9 of 1959
Look for: Remnants of a possible "D" Mint mark showing as a "bar" within the second "9" of the date.

VALUE:

Extra Fine	About Uncirculated	Uncirculated
5.00	12.00	25.00

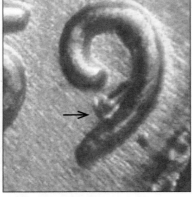

Listing Numbers
Wexler: WRPM-001

This variety is in dispute amongst experts. Some believe the variation is the result of probable die damage. However, it still commands a significant premium due to demand from those who accept it as an RPM variety.

COIN COURTESY OF: Brian Ribar

PHOTO COURTESY OF: Brian Allen

1960-D Large Date   Repunched Mint Mark

Look at: The D below the date
Look for: A very bold and wide Second D to the left.

VALUE:

Extra Fine	About Uncirculated	Uncirculated
2.00	2.75	12.00

Listing Numbers
CONECA: RPM-001
Potter:VCR#4/RPM#2
Wexler: WRPM-001

1960-D Large Date   Repunched Mint Mark

Look at: The D Mint mark below the date
Look for: Two additional D Mint marks protruding from the top-left portion of the D.

VALUE:

Extra Fine	About Uncirculated	Uncirculated
15.00	45.00	75.00

Listing Numbers
CONECA: RPM-004
Wexler: WRPM-001

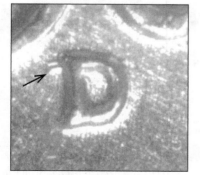

This variety may be difficult to identify in lower grades. Use good lighting and tilt the coin in various positions until you are able to view the remnant of a "D." It will be evident to the west of the upper portion of the primary "D".

COIN COURTESY OF: Brian Allen   *PHOTO COURTESY OF: Brian Allen*

1960-D Large Date   Repunched Mint Marks

Look at: The D below the date
Look for: Secondary D's in various locations

VALUE:	*(Average Values)*	
Extra Fine	**About Uncirculated**	**Uncirculated**
1.00	2.00	7.00

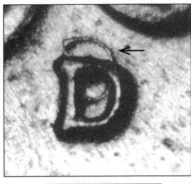

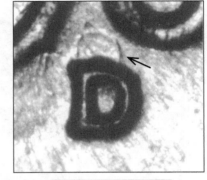

Listing Numbers
CONECA: RPM-013
Potter:VCR#5/RPM#3
Wexler: WRPM-003

Listing Numbers
CONECA: RPM-019
Potter:VCR#6/RPM#4
Wexler: WRPM-004

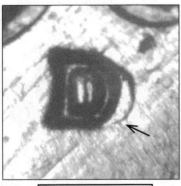

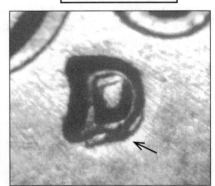

Listing Numbers
CONECA: RPM-023
Potter:VCR#7/RPM#5
Wexler: WRPM-006

Listing Numbers
CONECA: RPM-049
Potter:VCR#8/RPM#6
Wexler: WRPM-040

COINS COURTESY OF: Ken Potter   *PHOTOS COURTESY OF: Ken Potter*

*There are over 200 Repunched Mint marks for the 1960D Lincoln Cent and most are minor.
The coins shown above are commonly encountered and easily detected. Minor Repunched
Mint marks normally command less but are worth saving when found.*

1960-D   Repunched Mint Mark and Doubled Die

Look At: D below the Date, and 960 of the 1960
Look For: A "D" to the North that is nearly separated from the primary D.
Look for smaller numbers directly on top of the larger number of the 960.

VALUE:

Extra Fine	About Uncirculated	Uncirculated
12.00	25.00	100.00

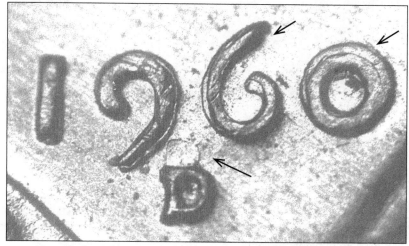

An easily detectable variety with a smaller 960 visible over the larger numbers.
You will easily see the doubled D widely separated from the main D as well.

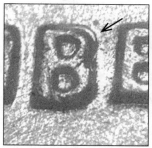 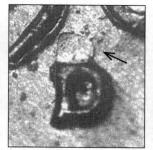 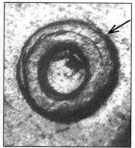

Doubling is also present on the top portion of the B in LIBERTY	*The secondary D between the 96 of the date.*	*A view of the small 0 of the date over the top of the larger 0.*

Listing Numbers
Breen#2232   Cherrypickers':FS-025.5   CONECA: RPM-100/DDO-001
Potter:VCR#3/RPM#1/DDO#1   Wexler: WRPM-103/WDDO-001

COIN COURTESY OF: Brian Ribar   *PHOTO COURTESY OF: Brian Allen*

Look at: The D below the date
Look for: A secondary D clearly visible west of the primary "D".

VALUE:

Extra Fine	About Uncirculated	Uncirculated
4.00	6.00	15.00

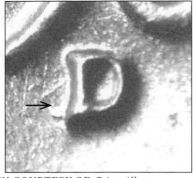

The D protruding to the West is actually rotated 90 degrees in a clockwise direction.

> **Listing Numbers**
> Breen#2237
> CONECA: RPM-001
> Potter:VCR#1/RPM#1
> Wexler: WRPM-001

1961-D   **Repunched Mint Mark**

Look at: The D below the date
Look for: A thin D that will be tilted and protruding from the left side of the primary D.

VALUE:

Extra Fine	About Uncirculated	Uncirculated
1.00	8.00	30.00

The secondary D can been seen in the middle loop of the main D and well to the West without high power magnification.

> **Listing Numbers**
> CONECA: RPM-057
> Potter:VCR#2/RPM#2
> Wexler: WRPM-085

COIN COURTESY OF: Brian Allen　　　*PHOTO COURTESY OF: Brian Allen*

Look at: The date, nose, tie and TRUST

Look for: Strong doubling on 1962, a doubled nose, bowtie and doubled letters of TRUST.

VALUE:

Extra Fine	About Uncirculated	Uncirculated
9.00	15.00	30.00

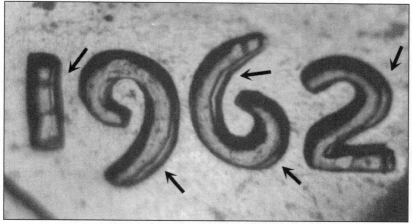

Very bold doubling to the right exists on the numbers of the date.

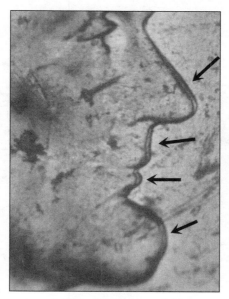

A clearly doubled nose and chin

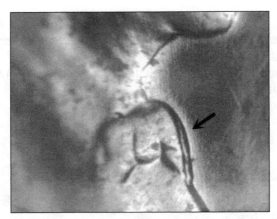

Nice doubling seen as second line on Lincoln's bowtie below the chin

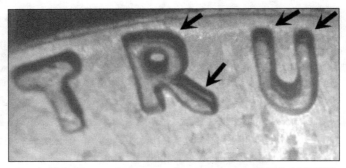

Very bold doubling on the letters to the top and right of TRU of TRUST

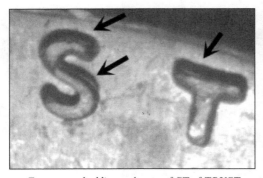

Easy to see doubling on letters of ST of TRUST

Listing Numbers
CONECA: DDO-001
Potter:VCR#1/DDO#1
Wexler: WDDO-001

1963-D

Doubled Die Obverse

Look at: The 3 of 1963
Look for: Traces of an additional "3" evident above and below the lower loop of the primary "3".

VALUE:

Extra Fine	About Uncirculated	Uncirculated
3.75	6.00	15.00

Listing Numbers
Breen#2241
Cherrypickers':FS-025.8
CONECA: DDO-001
Potter:VCR#1/DDO#1
Wexler: WDDO-001

COIN COURTESY OF: Ken Potter   *PHOTO COURTESY OF: Ken Potter*

1964

Doubled Die Obverse

Look at: L of LIBERTY and IN GOD on obverse.
Look for: A light "spike" rising from the top of the vertical bar of the L of LIBERTY.

VALUE:

Extra Fine	About Uncirculated	Uncirculated
4.75	8.00	15.00

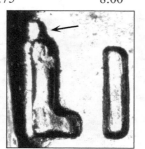

Listing Numbers
CONECA: DDO-022 Wexler: WDDO-007

PHOTO COURTESY OF: John Wexler

Look at: UNITED STATES OF AMERICA and E PLURIBUS UNUM on the reverse.

Look for: Strong doubling on UNITED STATES OF AMERICA and large "notches" on the top portions of the letters in E PLURIBUS UNUM.

VALUE:

Extra Fine	About Uncirculated	Uncirculated
20.00	30.00	90.00

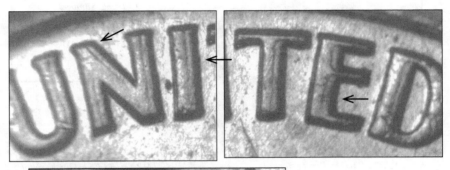

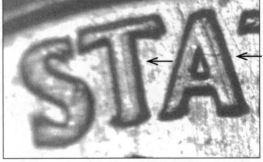

All letters of UNITED STATES show strong doubling to the east.

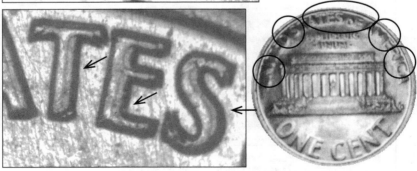

The strong doubling is clearly evident on the right side of the letters on UNITED STATES OF AMERICA.

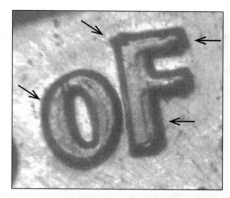
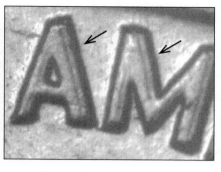

UNITED STATES OF AMERICA features strong doubling visible to the right.

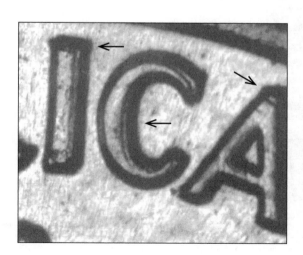

Listing Numbers
Breen#2242
Cherrypickers':FS-026
CONECA: DDR-001
Potter:VCR#1/DDR#1
Wexler: WDDR-001

COIN COURTESY OF: Kevin Flynn   *PHOTO COURTESY OF: Ken Potter*

Look at: UNITED STATES OF AMERICA and ONE CENT on reverse.
Look for: Strong doubling on UNITED STATES OF AMERICA and ONE CENT.

VALUE:

Extra Fine	About Uncirculated	Uncirculated
25.00	40.00	100.00

Listing Numbers
Cherrypickers':FS-027
CONECA: DDR-058
Potter:VCR#2/DDR#2
Wexler: WDDR-008

Very noticeable doubling on AMERICA spread toward the rim.

You can detect doubling on the bottom of the O and N of ONE in ONE CENT.

PHOTO COURTESY OF: Kevin Flynn/John Wexler

Look at: The FG, STATES OF AMERICA on the Reverse
Look for: Doubled FG and very thick letters (with separation lines) on
UNITED STATES OF AMERICA.

VALUE:

Extra Fine	About Uncirculated	Uncirculated
15.00	30.00	150.00

Very noticeable doubling of the FG near the right bottom of the Memorial

Thick letters of UNITED STATE of AMERICA. Notice the separation lines and the strong notch on the bottom bar of the E in AMERICA.

Listing Numbers
Cherrypickers':FS-027.4
CONECA: DDR-001
Potter:VCR#2/DDR#1
Wexler: WDDR-001

COIN COURTESY OF: Eric Axtell   *PHOTO COURTESY OF: Brian Allen*

1968-D Repunched Mint Mark

Look at: The "D" below the Date.
Look for: A strong vertical bar of a secondary "D" is west of the main "D".

VALUE:

Extra Fine	About Uncirculated	Uncirculated
2.00	5.00	20.00

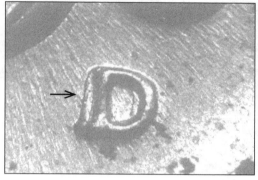

Listing Numbers
Cherrypickers':FS-027.3
CONECA: RPM-001
Potter:VCR#1/RPM#1
Wexler: WRPM-001

1969-S Reverse Counter-Clash

Look at: On the reverse between STATES and PLURIBUS
Look for: Raised letters of UNUM.

VALUE:

Extra Fine	About Uncirculated	Uncirculated
35.00	100.00	275.00

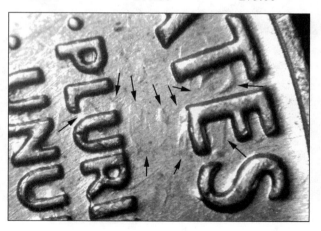

Listing Numbers
Wexler: WCC-001

COIN COURTESY OF: GJ Lawson   *PHOTO COURTESY OF: Brian Allen*

Look at: 1969, LIBERTY, and IN GOD WE TRUST
Look for: Very Dramatic secondary images on all letters of IN GOD WE TRUST, LIBERTY, and 1969.

VALUE:

Extra Fine	About Uncirculated	Uncirculated
12,000.00	25,000.00	42,000-58,000.00

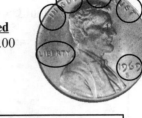

Listing Numbers
Breen#2252
Cherrypickers':FS-028
CONECA: DDO-001
Potter:VCR#1/DDO#1
Wexler: WDDO-001

PHOTO COURTESY OF: JT Stanton

BEWARE OF COUNTERFEITS AND MACHINE DOUBLING!

Look at: The D below 1970.
Look for: Secondary D's in various positions (two different varieties shown).

VALUE:

Extra Fine	About Uncirculated	Uncirculated
2.50	4.75	12.00

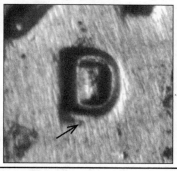

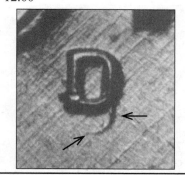

Listing Numbers	*Listing Numbers*
CONECA: RPM-001 Potter:VCR#1/RPM#1 Wexler: WRPM-001	CONECA: RPM-001 Potter:VCR#2/ RPM#2 Wexler: WRPM-001

1970-D

Doubled Die Obverse

Look at: 1970-D Lincoln Cents.
Look for: Doubled numbers of the date as seen below.

VALUE:

Extra Fine	About Uncirculated	Uncirculated
2.50	3.75	10.00

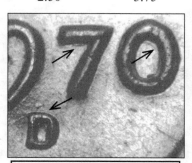

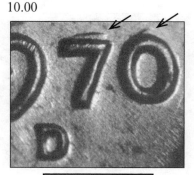

Listing Numbers	*Listing Numbers*
CONECA: RPM-006 Wexler: WRPM-005/WDDO-003	Wexler: WDDO-018

COINS COURTESY OF: Brian Allen   *PHOTOS COURTESY OF: Brian Allen*

Look at: The S below 1970.
Look for: Secondary S's in various positions.

VALUE:

Extra Fine	About Uncirculated	Uncirculated
2.50	4.75	12.00

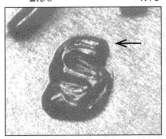

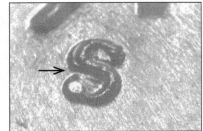

Listing Numbers
CONECA: RPM-001
Potter:VCR#3/RPM#1
Wexler: WRPM-001

Listing Numbers
CONECA: RPM-002
Potter:VCR#4/RPM#2
Wexler: WRPM-002

1970-S

Doubled Die Obverse

Look at: The 70 of the 1970.
Look for: A secondary loop of the 0 below the primary 0 and a light line underneath the horizontal bar of the 7 in 1970.

VALUE:

Extra Fine	About Uncirculated	Uncirculated
2.50	3.75	10.00

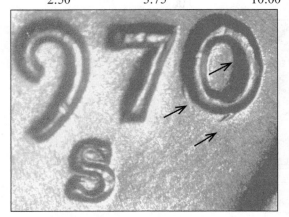

The doubling on the bottom of the 0 may be a complete outline of another 0 or can be seen as a small line under the 0. The full outline will bring higher prices than those listed above.

Listing Numbers
Breen#2257
Cherrypickers': FS-030.1
CONECA: DDO-005
Potter:VCR#6/DDO#2
Wexler: WDDO-009

COIN COURTESY OF: Brian Allen   *PHOTO COURTESY OF: Brian Allen*

Look at: 0 of 1970, LIBERTY, and IN GOD WE TRUST.
Look for: Very strong doubling on "0" of date, IN GOD WE TRUST.
LIBE of LIBERTY; light on 197 of date, and RTY of LIBERTY.

VALUE:

Extra Fine	About Uncirculated	Uncirculated
3,500.00	4,800.00	12,000-30,000.00

Listing Numbers
Breen#2255
Cherrypickers': FS-029
CONECA: DDO-001
Potter:VCR#5/DDO#1
Wexler: WDDO-001

Beware of the strike doubling that is evident of many 1968-1973 Lincoln Cents.

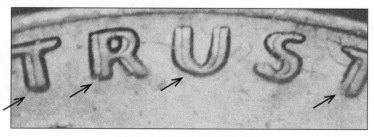

PHOTO COURTESY OF: JT Stanton

Look at: The 970 of the date and the TY of LIBERTY.

Look for: Top of 7 is level with the top of the 9 and 0 of date and the 7 has a shorter leg in comparison to the Low 7. Look for much shorter "arms" on the T and Y of LIBERTY.

VALUE:

Extra Fine	About Uncirculated	Uncirculated
8.00	12.00	30.00

On the "Small Date" the top of the 7 is level with the 9 and 0 in the date.

Listing Numbers
Breen#2256
Cherrypickers': FS-:030.2
Potter:VCR#2/ODV#1

The 1970S Small Date (left photo) will have a weak TY of LIBERTY when compared to a Large S LIBERTY (right photo).

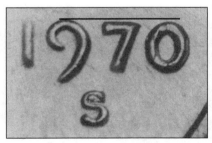
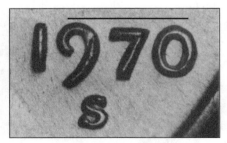

Side by Side Comparison of the Small (left) and Large Dates (right) will show the Large Date has a Lower 7 that is not even with the 9 and 0 of the date. The photo on the left is the valuable variety.

COIN COURTESY OF: Gary Kelly   PHOTO COURTESY OF: Ken Potter

Look at: IN GOD WE TRUST, LIBERTY, and DATE.
Look for: Strong doubling on IN GOD WE TRUST and very strong doubling of LIBERTY.

VALUE:

Extra Fine	About Uncirculated	Uncirculated
30.00	45.00	100.00

Only slight separation is visible on the 1971 and IN of IN GOD

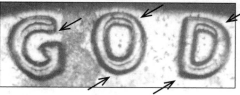 

Very noticeable doubling on GOD WE TRUST

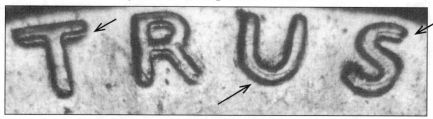

The most dramatic doubling is clearly visible on LIBERTY

The most dramatic doubling is clearly visible on LIBERTY

Listing Numbers
Breen#-2260
CONECA: DDO-001
Wexler: WDDO-001

Cherrypickers':FS-031
Potter:VCR#1DDO#1

COIN COURTESY OF: Ken Potter   *PHOTO COURTESY OF: Ken Potter*

Look at: IN GOD WE TRUST.
Look for: Doubling on IN GOD WE TRUST.

VALUE:

Extra Fine	About Uncirculated	Uncirculated
30.00	45.00	70.00

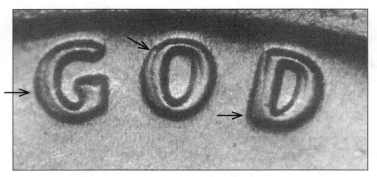

Slight doubling on the left side of the letters in GOD

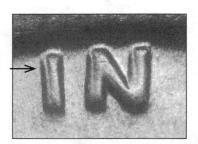

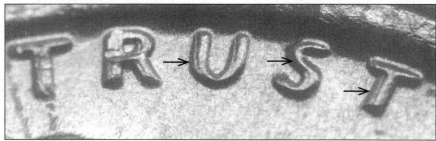

TRUST features doubling like IN GOD WE to the left of the letters.

Listing Numbers

CONECA: DDO-002	Potter:VCR#2/DDO#2	Wexler: WDDO-002

COIN COURTESY OF: Brian Allen   *PHOTO COURTESY OF: Brian Allen*

Look at: IN GOD WE TRUST.
Look for: Secondary images on all lettering of
IN GOD WE TRUST

VALUE:

Extra Fine	About Uncirculated	Uncirculated
25.00	45.00	100.00

Nice doubling seen on all letter of
IN GOD WE TRUST

This doubled die is proving to be very scarce

Listing Numbers

CONECA: DDO-001	Potter:VCR#1/DDO#1	Wexler: WDDO-001

COIN COURTESY OF: Larry Comer   *PHOTO COURTESY OF: Ken Potter*

Look at: 1972 LIBERTY and IN GOD WE TRUST.
Look for: Very dramatic doubling on IN GOD WE TRUST, LIBERTY, and date.

VALUE:

Extra Fine	About Uncirculated	Uncirculated
80.00	145.00	420.00

You cannot miss the doubling of the date on this coin!   *Strong doubling on IN*

There are 10-1972 Doubled Obverses, although not as strong as the #1 the others are all easily detected!

Very wide doubling on the letters of IN GOD WE TRUST

___

Listing Numbers
Breen#2265
Cherrypickers':FS-033.3
CONECA: DDO-001
Potter:VCR#1/DDO#1
Wexler: WDDO-001

VERY strong doubling of IN GOD WE TRUST

Very Bold and strong doubling on LIBERTY

Look at: 1972, LIBERTY, and IN GOD WE TRUST.
Look for: Doubling on IN GOD WE TRUST, LIBERTY, and light doubling on the date.

VALUE:

Extra Fine	About Uncirculated	Uncirculated
6.00	15.00	35.00

Nice doubling on the date.

VERY strong doubling to the North on LIBERTY.

Doubling to the east on IN GOD WE TRUST VERY strong on all lettering of IN GOD WE TRUST.

Doubling to the east on IN GOD WE TRUST VERY strong on all lettering of IN GOD WE TRUST.

Listing Numbers
Cherrypickers':FS-033.52   CONECA: DDO-002
Potter:VCR#2/DDO#2   Wexler: WDDO-002

PHOTO COURTESY OF: Ken Potter

Look at: 1972, LIBERTY, and IN GOD WE TRUST.
Look for: Doubling on IN GOD WE TRUST, LIBERTY. and the date.

VALUE:

Extra Fine	About Uncirculated	Uncirculated
6.00	15.00	35.00

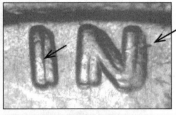

Only slight doubling visible on the 972 of the date.

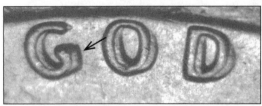

Nice doubling on IN GOD WE TRUST .

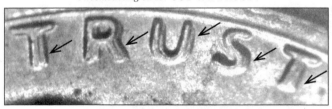

Very nice doubling on TRUST.

Very bold separation of the LIBER of LIBERTY.

Listing Numbers	
Cherrypickers':FS-033.57	CONECA: DDO-007
Potter:VCR#7/DDO#7	Wexler: WDDO-007

COIN COURTESY OF: Kevin Flynn   *PHOTO COURTESY OF: Ken Potter*

Look at: IN GOD WE TRUST, LIBERTY, and 1972.
Look for: Doubling on IN GOD WE TRUST, LIBERTY, and on 72 of 1972.

VALUE:

Extra Fine	About Uncirculated	Uncirculated
8.00	10.00	20.00

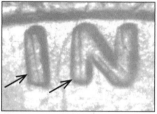 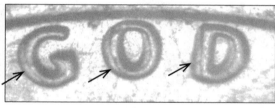

Doubling of the date is most evident on the "72".

IN GOD WE TRUST is an easy location to spot the doubling. Notice the strong doubling on the west side of letters.

Listing Numbers
Cherrypickers': FS-033.58
CONECA: DDO-008
Potter:VCR#8/DDO#8
Wexler: WDDO-008

Obvious doubling is visible on the LIBE of LIBERTY.

COIN COURTESY OF: Kevin Flynn   *PHOTO COURTESY OF: Ken Potter*

Look at: IN GOD WE TRUST, LIBERTY, and 1972.
Look for: Doubling on IN GOD WE TRUST, LIBERTY, and 72 of 1972.

VALUE:

Extra Fine	About Uncirculated	Uncirculated
8.00	15.00	30.00

Notice the separation lines on the bottom bar of the L and in the loops of the B.

Listing Numbers
CONECA: DDO-001
Potter:VCR#1/DDO#1
Wexler: WDDO-001

Strong doubling on the W of WE and slightly visible on the vertical bar of the E.

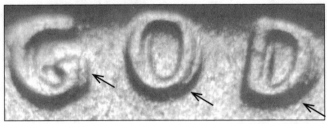

The strongest doubling is present on the letters of GOD and TRUST.

COIN COURTESY OF: Ken Potter   *PHOTO COURTESY OF: Ken Potter*

Look at: IN GOD WE TRUST, LIBERTY, and 1972.
Look for: Doubling on IN GOD WE TRUST, LIBERTY, and slightly on the inside of the 2 of 1972.

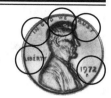

VALUE:

Extra Fine	About Uncirculated	Uncirculated
35.00	50.00	100.00

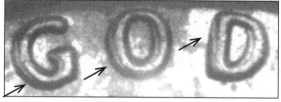

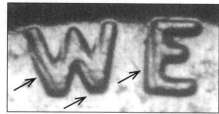

Listing Numbers
Potter:VCR#1/DDO#1
Wexler: WDDO-006

Look closely at the vertical portions of the letters of IN GOD WE TRUST; you can see the separation lines.

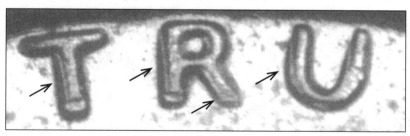

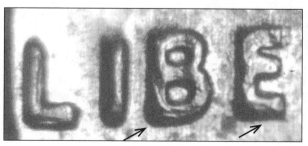

Slightly visible doubling is present on the bottom of the LIBE and on the top inside loop of the 2 in 1972.

COIN COURTESY OF: Bill and Debbie Rourke   *PHOTO COURTESY OF: Ken Potter*

A WORD OF CAUTION-Master Die Doubling

It should be noted that Lincoln Cents dated 1972, from all three Mints, are known with a "Master Doubled Die." While they are true doubled dies, the term "Master" indicates that their point of origin is somewhere in the Master Tools (and in most cases will be common).

In this case the "Master Die" was hub doubled during its manufacture (in the same manner in which a working die) and then the doubling was transferred at the next stage when it was used to produce the working hub(s) in turn transferred the doubling to many working dies. This scenario resulted in many working dies bearing the identical doubled die variety. Some of these dies were kept in-house at the Philadelphia "Mother Mint" (and bear no Mint mark) while others were Mint marked and shipped to the Denver and San Francisco branch Mints.

This Master Doubled Die is common and carries no extra value.

OTHER 1972 DOUBLED DIES

LIBERTY is the easiest location to locate the doubling. Look at the top of the bar of the L and the upper loops of the B and R of LIBERTY.

Notice the notch on the upper portion of the D and the left side of the bar of E in WE.

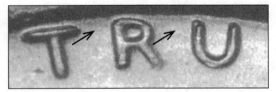

The Master Die Doubling is noticeable on the upper portions of the TRU of TRUST on the obverse of the coin.

While we only show four doubled dies on the 1972 Cent, it should be noted that a number of other doubled die varieties exist for this date for all three Mints. All, except the Master Doubled Die described above, have values starting at about $10 and ranging up to about $50 and more; they are considered to be of fair to high interest to collectors and are very marketable!

If you find one that is not a perfect match for the four shown in this book we recommend that you consult more detailed guides (listed on page 211) or seek out a professional attributer. Don't be afraid to ask!

1980

Look at: 1980 and LIBERTY.

Look for: Separation lines on this variety are most noticeable on 1980.

VALUE:

Extra Fine	About Uncirculated	Uncirculated
60.00	125.00	350.00

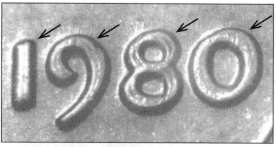

Notice the lines visible on the 1980.

Listing Numbers
Breen#2292
Cherrypickers': FS-034
CONECA: DDO-001
Potter:VCR#1/DDO#1
Wexler: WDDO-001

COIN COURTESY OF: Lonesome John   *PHOTO COURTESY OF: Ken Potter*

1982 Copper Large Date   Doubled Die Obverse

Look at: IN GOD WE TRUST and LIBERTY.

Look for: Doubling on IN GOD WE TRUST and slightly on the bottom of LIBE of LIBERTY.

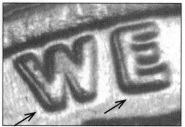

VALUE:

Extra Fine	About Uncirculated	Uncirculated
15.00	25.00	50.00

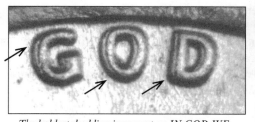

The boldest doubling is present on IN GOD WE.

Nice doubling on WE of WE TRUST.

Listing Numbers
Breen#2300   Cherrypickers':FS-034.5
CONECA: DDO-002   Potter:VCR#6/DDO#1
Wexler: WDDO-002

COIN COURTESY OF: Ken Potter   *PHOTO COURTESY OF: Ken Potter*

Look at: 1983 Lincoln Cents.
Look for: A 1983 cent struck on a solid copper alloy planchet vs. the normal copper plated zinc planchet.

VALUE:
Extra Fine   **About Uncirculated**   **Uncirculated**
Estimated $15,000 and up!!

Discovered While Searching Pocket Change!!

Since the solid copper alloy cents and copper plated zinc cents outwardly look virtually the same, finding one of these will be difficult, but the effort will be well worth it if you do find one. While some die-hard Lincoln cent specialists can visually discern the difference between a high percentage of the solid alloy coins vs. the copper plated cents by color and striking characteristics alone, this is unreliable. Weighing every 1983 cent encountered on a good scale is the only sure-fire way to find one of these. The pre-1982 solid copper alloy pieces weigh 3.1 grams while a 1982 to current copper plated zinc core cent will weigh 2.5 grams. The rarity we are seeking is a 1983 cent struck on a solid copper alloy planchet left over from a previous year and struck in error. If it is the error, it will weigh 3.1 grams. Professional authentication is a must.

COIN COURTESY OF: Billy G. Crawford   *PHOTO COURTESY OF: Billy G. Crawford*

Look at: IN GOD WE TRUST and LIBERTY.
Look for: Doubling on IN GOD WE TRUST and on the bottom of LIBE of LIBERTY.

VALUE:

Extra Fine	About Uncirculated	Uncirculated
15.00	20.00	75.00

Notice the separation lines on the bottom of the L, top and middle of the B and R of LIBERTY.

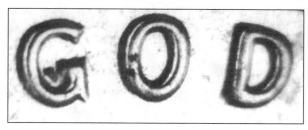

IN GOD WE TRUST features significant doubling that is easily detected.

Listing Numbers
Breen#2309
Cherrypickers': FS-035
CONECA: DDO-001
Potter:VCR#2/DDO#1
Wexler: WDDO-001

COIN COURTESY OF: Ken Potter

PHOTO COURTESY OF: Ken Potter

Look at: E PLURIBUS UNUM, UNITED STATES, and ONE CENT.
Look for: Doubling on UNITED STATES of
AMERICA and ONE CENT.

VALUE:

Extra Fine	About Uncirculated	Uncirculated
55.00	80.00	300.00

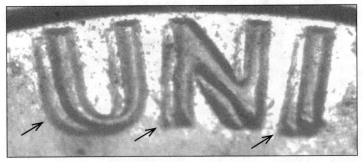

The bold doubling of the letters of UNITED.

*ED of UNITED with
bold doubled letters.*

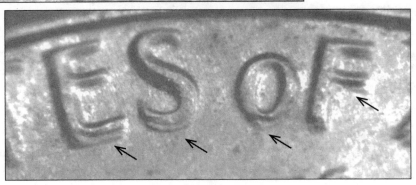

Doubling on ES and OF.

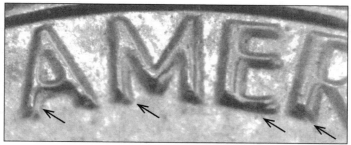

Strong doubled letters of AMER in AMERICA.

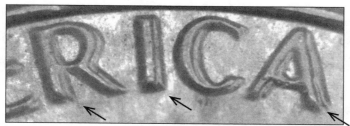

The remaining letters in AMERICA.

Nearly complete separation on the letters of E PLURIBUS UNUM.

Again more doubling. The doubling can be located on the entire reverse.
This variety is well known and popular.

Listing Numbers		
Breen#2310	Cherrypickers':FS-036	CONECA: DDR-001
Potter:VCR#1/DDR#1	Wexler: WDDR-001	

COIN COURTESY OF: Mickey Smith   *PHOTO COURTESY OF: Brian Allen*

Look at: The letters of E. PLURIBUS UNUM and UNITED STATES OF AMERICA.

Look for: Strong doubling of all letters.

VALUE:

Extra Fine	About Uncirculated	Uncirculated
55.00	80.00	150.00

Strong doubling is visible on all lettering of the reverse

Listing Numbers
Wexler: WDDR-002
Potter:VCR#8/DDR#2

The 1983 Doubled Die Reverse #2 shows less doubling than the Doubled Die Obverse #1, seen on the previous page. However, Doubled Die Reverse #2 is much scarcer though still possible to find in pocket change with diligent searching.

Look at: 1983, LIBERTY, and bottom on the reverse of the coin.
Look for: An upside down IBE rising from the date, a bold LIBE on the bottom LIBERTY, and a large break on the reverse over ONE CENT.

VALUE:

Extra Fine	**About Uncirculated**	**Uncirculated**
100.00	200.00	750.00

Portions of LIBERTY can be seen in the field directly above the date.

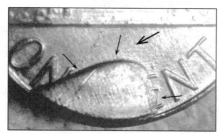

The large break on the reverse makes this variety easy to locate without the assistance of magnification.

A boldly damaged LIBERTY with the visible remains of the counter clash rim (the long circular lines).

Listing Numbers	
Cherrypickers':FS-035.3	Wexler: WCLO-001
Potter:VCR#6/CDO#1	

COIN COURTESY OF: GJ Lawson   *PHOTO COURTESY OF: Brian Allen*

1983 Counter Clash "Extra Letters in Motto"

Look at: Below IN GOD of IN GOD WE TRUST.
Look for: Portions of another N and GOD below IN GOD.

VALUE:

Extra Fine	About Uncirculated	Uncirculated
20.00	60.00	120.00

Visible remains of IN GOD can be seen in the areas directly below the IN GO of IN GOD WE TRUST

Listing Numbers
Potter:VCR#1/CLO#2
Wexler: WCLO-002

COIN COURTESY OF: Brian Allen　　　　*PHOTO COURTESY OF: Brian Allen*

1983 Doubled Die Obverse

Look at: The date of 1983.
Look for: Secondary images to the south on the 983 of 1983.

VALUE:

Extra Fine	About Uncirculated	Uncirculated
15.00	30.00	80.00

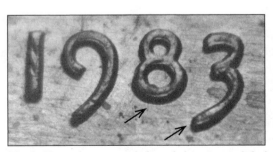

The doubling is best seen with the underlying image shifted south on 983.

Listing Numbers
Breen#2309
Cherrypickers': FS-035.1
CONECA: DDO-002
Potter:VCR#4/DDO#2
Wexler: WDDO-002

COIN COURTESY OF: Ken Potter　　　　*PHOTO COURTESY OF: Ken Potter*

Look at: Ear, beard and lapel.
Look for: A second earlobe to the South of the primary ear.

VALUE:

Extra Fine	About Uncirculated	Uncirculated
65.00	100.00	250.00

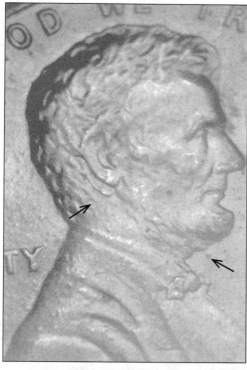

Listing Numbers
Breen#2314
Cherrypickers': FS-037
CONECA: DDO-001
Potter:VCR#1/DDO#1
Wexler: WDDO-001

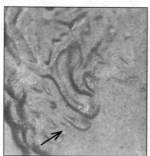

Doubled Ear   Normal Ear

COIN COURTESY OF: Brian Allen   *PHOTO COURTESY OF: Brian Allen*

Look at: Ear, chin and beard.

Look for: A second earlobe, slightly to the South of the primary earlobe and a very boldly doubled chin.

VALUE:

Extra Fine	About Uncirculated	Uncirculated
55.00	70.00	100.00

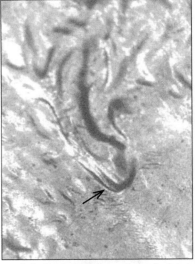

A slight division line seen to the south of the primary ear.

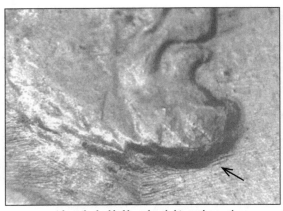

A heavily doubled beard and chin to the south.

Listing Numbers
Potter:VCR#3/DDO#3
Wexler: WDDO-008

COIN COURTESY OF: Frank Baumann　　　*PHOTO COURTESY OF: Brian Allen*

Look at: The date, LIBERTY and IN GOD WE TRUST, base of bust and top of Lincoln's head.

Look for: Strong doubling on Lincoln's head, IN GOD WE TRUST and the date.

VALUE:

Extra Fine	About Uncirculated	Uncirculated
25.00	40.00	70.00

Listing Numbers
Cherrypickers': FS-038
CONECA: DDO-002
Potter: VCR#2/DDO#2
Wexler: WDDO-005

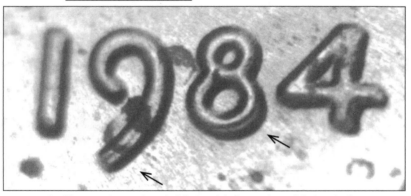

Doubling is evident on the tail of the 9 and the bottom loop of the 8 in the date

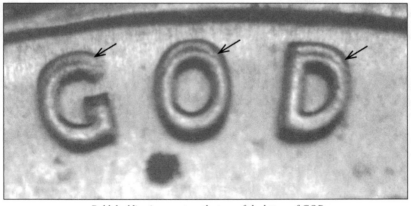

Bold doubling is present on the tops of the letters of GOD

COIN COURTESY OF: Ken Potter   *PHOTO COURTESY OF: Ken Potter*

Look at: D Mint Marks below the dates of 1985D, 1986D, 1987D, 1988D, and 1989D Lincoln Cents.
Look for: Various Repunched Mint Marks.

VALUE:

Extra Fine	About Uncirculated	Uncirculated
7.00	15.00	25.00

    Repunched Mint Marks on these years have been particularly elusive as the few varieties created have been lost in the huge mintages of the era, like a "needle in a haystack." The $10-$35 values that any of them command — even in circulated grades — is reason enough to seek them out from pocket change.

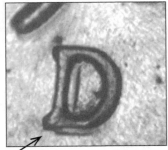

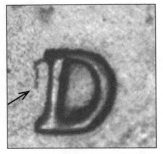

1985-D WRPM-001/RPM-001   11 different 1985-D RPM's known   1985-D WRPM-007/RPM-005

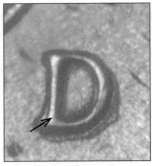

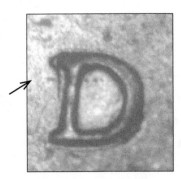

1986-D WRPM-003/RPM-007
13 Different RPMs known for
1986-D

1987-D RPM-007/ RPM-012
15 different Doubled Mint
Marks known for 1987-D.

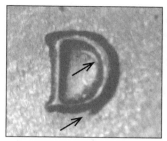

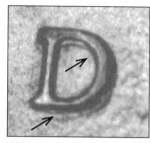

1987-D WRPM-004/RPM-004

1987-D WRPM-011/RPM-006

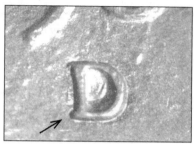

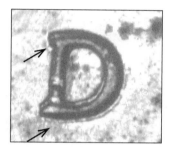

1987-D WRPM-001
COIN COURTESY OF: Eric Axtell

1988-D WRPM-9/RPM-001
7 different Doubled Mint
Marks known.

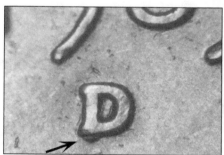

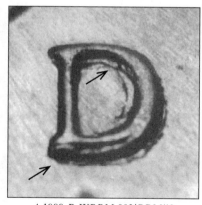

This is a 1983-D/D Lincoln Cent that was found in pocket change by Brian Allen just before this book went to print. A find like the above could net you $10-$15.
This RPM is listed as WRPM-006

A 1989-D WRPM-002/RPM#9
10 RPMs known for 1989-D
PHOTO COURTESY OF: Ken Potter

PHOTOS COURTESY OF: Brian Allen

Look at: Between the 1 and 9 of the 1987.
Look for: A horizontal D punched directly between the 19 of 1987.

VALUE:

Extra Fine	About Uncirculated	Uncirculated
45.00	75.00	150.00

The exact nature of this variety is in dispute amongst specialists. Some believe its classification is unproven or that it is the result of less significant causes. Nonetheless, it still commands a significant premium amongst proponent of the variety.

Listing Numbers
Wexler: WRPM-014

COIN COURTESY OF: *Brian Allen*   PHOTO COURTESY OF: *Brian Allen*

Look at: The letters AM of AMERICA and FG.
Look for: A very close AM of AMERICA as those seen on 1994-2002.

VALUE:

	Extra Fine	About Uncirculated	Uncirculated
1992	Estimates	2,000.00++	3,000.00++
1992-D	600.00	1,000.00	2,000.00+

VERY RARE! The AM of AMERICA *will be* touching at the
bottom of the letters in this very rare variety. Examples are seldom
seen for sale and premiums continue to climb.

*Normal Appearing Reverse
AMERICA for the 1992-D
Lincoln Cent. This variety, with
the "CLOSE AM."*

Listing Numbers	
Potter:VCR#1/#1	FS: 1c-1992D-901

COIN COURTESY OF: Colin Kusch   *PHOTO COURTESY OF: Ken Potter*

Look at: Between the last three columns on the Memorial Building on the reverse.

Look for: A nearly complete column in last bay and partial column in the bottom of the 2nd to last bay.

VALUE:

Extra Fine	About Uncirculated	Uncirculated
85.00	250.00	550.00

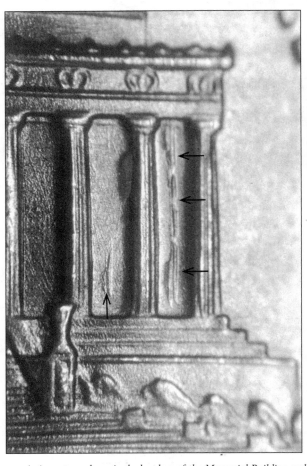

Listing Numbers
Cherrypickers': FS-039.9
CONECA: DDR-001
Potter:VCR#1/DDR#1
Wexler: WDDR-006

A nice extra column in the last bay of the Memorial Building and the partial remains of another in the second to last Memorial Building Bay. This variety is relatively new and highly desired by collectors. This variety is visible without the assistance of magnification; however, magnification is recommended.

COIN COURTESY OF: Brian Allen   *PHOTO COURTESY OF: Brian Allen*

Look at: Between the last three columns on the Memorial Building on the reverse.

Look for: A nearly complete column in last bay and partial column in the bottom of the 2nd to last bay.

VALUE:

Extra Fine	About Uncirculated	Uncirculated
80.00	180.00	350.00

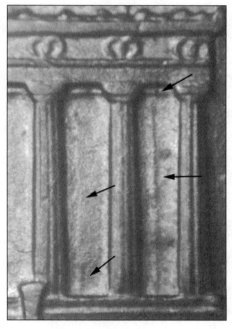

Very similar to the 1994 1c listed on the previous page.

Listing Numbers	
Potter:VCR#3/DDR#3	Wexler: WDDR-007
Crawford: CDDR-009	CONECA: DDR-002

COIN COURTESY OF: Brian Allen   *PHOTO COURTESY OF: Brian Allen*

Look at: LIBERTY and IN GOD WE TRUST.
Look for: Bold doubling on LIBERTY and IN GOD WE TRUST.

VALUE:

Extra Fine	About Uncirculated	Uncirculated
12.50	20.00	45.00

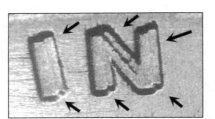

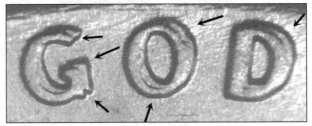

Wide separation is seen on LIBERTY and IN GOD WE TRUST.

Listing Numbers
Cherrypickers': FS-040
CONECA: DDO-001
Potter:VCR#1/DDO#1
Wexler: WDDO-001

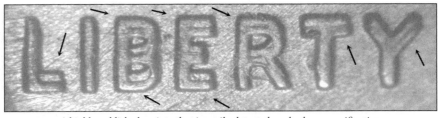

A highly published variety that is easily detected under low magnification.

COIN COURTESY OF: Mickey Smith   *PHOTO COURTESY OF: Brian Allen*

Look at: GOD WE TRUST, date, and the D below the date.
Look for: Bold doubling of GOD WE TRUST, doubling of the date, and a boldly doubled D Mint mark.

VALUE:

Extra Fine	About Uncirculated	Uncirculated
125.00	200.00	500.00

The doubling on the D is very prominent and easy to locate.

Slight doubling is visible on the right side of IN.

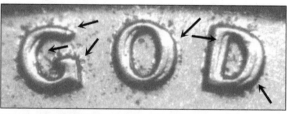

Very bold doubling on GOD is easy to pick up.

Listing Numbers
Cherrypickers': FS-041
CONECA: DDO-003
Potter:VCR#1/DDO#3
Wexler: WDDO-003

Extremely bold separation on the letters of WE TRUST.

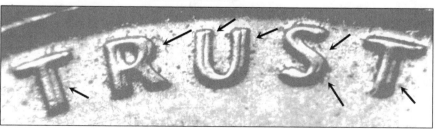

COIN COURTESY OF: Russ LeBeau   *PHOTO COURTESY OF: Brian Allen*

Look at: WE TRUST and date.

Look for: Doubling on WE TRUST, the date, and strong notches on the inside loops of the 996.

VALUE:

Extra Fine	About Uncirculated	Uncirculated
125.00	225.00	675.00

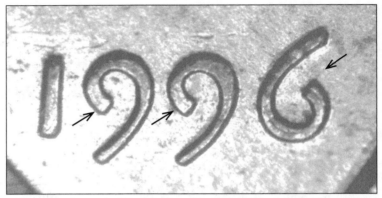

Strong notches on the 996 of the date with clearly visible separation lines on the upper loops of the 99 and the lower loop of the 6.

A nice shifting on the letters of TRUST with complete double lines visible.

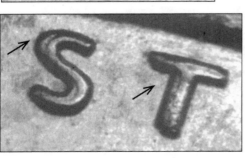

Listing Numbers
CONECA: Unknown
Potter:VCR#1/DDO#1
Wexler: WDDO-006?

COIN COURTESY OF: Russ LeBeau

PHOTO COURTESY OF: Brian Allen

Look at: Ear.

Look for: A second earlobe to the South of the primary lobe.

VALUE:

Extra Fine	About Uncirculated	Uncirculated
45.00	60.00	150.00

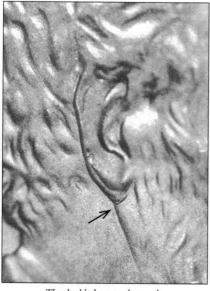

The doubled ear to the south.

There are at least 15 other locations to spot doubling on this doubled die!

All 15 areas of doubling can be seen highlighted in color at www.koinpro.com

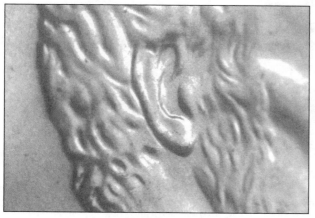

A normal 1997 Lincoln Cent ear.

COIN COURTESY OF: *Brian Allen*   PHOTO COURTESY OF: *Brian Allen*

Look at: The area directly below the date.
Look for: A faint image of a D (you may be required to tilt and rotate the coin at several angles to see the image).

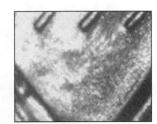

VALUE:

	Extra Fine	About Uncirculated	Uncirculated
1994	-	0.25	1.50
1997	0.10	0.25	2.00
1998	0.05	0.15	1.50
1999	-	4.25	8.00

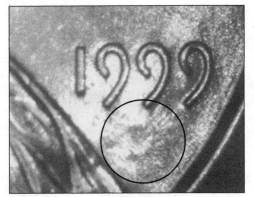

A close up of the very strong 1999 Phantom D.

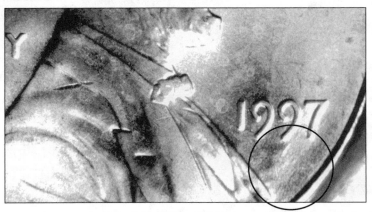

This variety is known on the 1994, 1997, 1998, and 1999 Lincoln Cents. It is possible that it may be found on other dates, none of which have been confirmed at the time of this writing. The "Phantom D" will appear on Philadelphia Cents and is the result of the Mint grinding away most of the "D" from the Master Die in order to make dies for Philadelphia (which bear no Mint Mark for cents). So-called "Phantom S's" have also been reported but have proven to be remnants of a weaker "Phantom D."

COIN S COURTESY OF: GJ Lawson   *PHOTOS COURTESY OF: Brian Allen*

1998, 1999 & 2000 W/Proof Style Reverses

Look at: The letters AM of AMERICA and designers initials, FG.
Look for: A "wider" gap between the lower portion of the AM of AMERICA; the FG closer to the base of the Memorial building.

VALUE:

	Extra Fine	About Uncirculated	Uncirculated
1998	4.00	15.00	50.00
1999	150.00	275.00	700.00 - 1,000.00+
2000	2.00	12.00	45.00

*The AM of AMERICA will **NOT** be touching on the valuable variety found in 1998, 1999, and 2000.*

Normal business strike with the letters of AM on AMERICA touching at the bottom of the letters.

For unknown reasons a normal circulation strike was produced using a reverse die intended for proof coins. Some enthusiasts report finding the "proof style reverse" on a 1997; however, the authors have not examined or verified any 1997 with a Proof Reverse. This variety could possibly exist on Lincoln Cents from 1994-2000. There are <u>no</u> Denver Mint Marks known with this variety.

COIN COURTESY OF: Brian Allen   PHOTO COURTESY OF: Brian Allen

1995, 1996, 1999 & 2000 — Misaligned Clashes

Look at: Various locations on the obverse.

Look for: Portions of a "rotated" or "misaligned" clash.

VALUE:	(With exception of the 1995 all prices are estimates)		
	Extra Fine	**About Uncirculated**	**Uncirculated**
1995	2.00	4.00	15.00
1996-TY 1	2.00	5.00	15.00
1996-TY 2	10.00	15.00	50.00
1999 TY 1	2.00	5.00	15.00
1999 TY II	2.00	5.00	15.00
2000	25.00	75.00	200.00

Portions of an "F" on the 1995.

Impression on 1996 TY I.

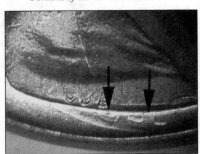
Remnant of "ST" on 1996 TY II.

Remnants of a "T" on 1999 TY1.

Impression on the 1999 TY II.

URIBUS below the bust on the 2000.

ALL PHOTOS COURTESY OF: Mike Diamond

Strike It Rich With Pocket Change

Look at: LIBERTY.
Look for: Very thick letters, notably RTY of LIBERTY.
VALUE:

Listing Numbers
CONECA: DDO-001
Crawford: CDDO-001
Potter:VCR#1/DDO#1
Wexler: WDDO-001

Extra Fine	About Uncirculated	Uncirculated
60.00	125.00	150.00 - 300.00

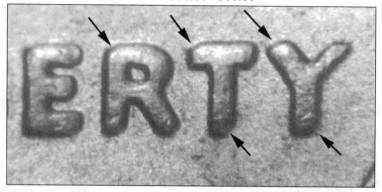

COIN COURTESY OF: Brian Allen   *PHOTO COURTESY OF: Brian Allen*

Look at: LIBERTY.
Look for: Slight notching on letters of LIBERTY.

VALUE:

Listing Numbers
CONECA: DDO-001
Crawford: CDDO-001
Potter:VCR#1/DDO#1
Wexler: WDDO-001

Extra Fine	About Uncirculated	Uncirculated
15.00	25.00	60.00 - 100.00

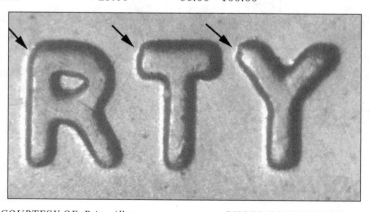

COIN COURTESY OF: Brian Allen   *PHOTO COURTESY OF: Brian Allen*

Look at: LIBERTY on obverse and UNITED STATES OF AMERICA on the reverse.

Look for: Slight notching on LIBERTY and very thick lettering on UNITED STATES OF AMERICA.

VALUE:

Extra Fine	About Uncirculated	Uncirculated
60.00	125.00	200.00 - 300.00

NOTE: Prices listed here are for "early die states." Late to middle die states command under one-half of these prices listed.

Slight notching visible on the bottom of ERTY of LIBERTY.

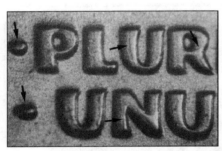
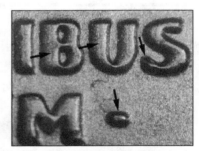

Extremely thick lettering and dots on E PLURIBUS UNUM and the TES of STATES

Listing Numbers
CONECA: DDR-001
Crawford: CDDO-002/CDDR-002
Potter:VCR#1/DDO#1
Wexler: WDDO-001/WDDR-001
FS: 1c-2004-801

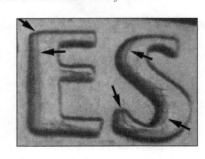

PHOTOS COURTESY OF: Billy G. Crawford

Look at: E PLURIBUS UNUM on the reverse.
Look for: Very thick lettering on E PLURIBUS UNUM with visible notching and separation lines.

VALUE:

Extra Fine	About Uncirculated	Uncirculated
10.00	15.00	40.00+

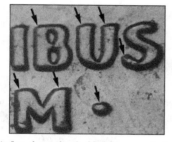 

At first glance this doubled die reverse looks nearly identical to the doubled reverse listed on the previous page. However, careful examination reveals two different varieties.

PHOTOS COURTESY OF: Billy G. Crawford

2004-D

Doubled Die Reverse

Look at: E PLURIBUS UNUM.
Look for: Doubling to the east of all letters on E PLURIBUS UNUM.

VALUE:

Extra Fine	About Uncirculated	Uncirculated
10.00	25.00	80.00

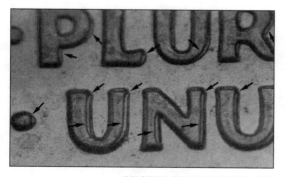

Listing Numbers
CONECA: DDR-001
Crawford: CDDR-005
Potter: VCR#1/DDO#1
Wexler: WDDR-001
FS: 2004-D-1c-801

PHOTOS COURTESY OF: Billy G. Crawford

JEFFERSON NICKEL VARIETIES

Composition: copper 75% and nickel 25%
Years: 1938-1942 and 1946-Present
Weight: 5 Grams
Diameter: 21.2mm

Composition: 35% silver, 56% copper and 9% manganese
Years: 1942-1945
Weight: 5 Grams
Diameter: 21.2mm

The "NEW" Jefferson Nickels (2004-2006)

President George W. Bush authorized the modification of all Jefferson Nickel coinage of 2004-2006 to commemorate the 200 hundred year anniversaries of the Louisiana Purchase and the Lewis and Clark expedition.

The "Westward Journey Nickel Series "began in 2004 with the regular President Thomas Jefferson obverse as used on previous issues with two separate reverse designs: the Peace Medal or "Hand-Shake" and Keelboat motifs. In 2005 a new portrait of Jefferson appears along with two new reverse designs that recognize the Native Americans and wildlife encountered by the Lewis and Clark expedition (epitomized by the Bison reverse) and the "Ocean in view! O! The joy!" reverse. The 2006 Nickels revert back to the familiar Monticello reverse design with a new obverse portrait of Jefferson facing forward for the first time.

A sample of each of the Westward Journey Nickels will be a nice addition to your coin collection and are worth searching for new varieties, but hoarding large quantities of the nickels will probably never materialize into a moneymaking investment. According to the US Mint the number of Jefferson Nickels produced from 2004-2006 will be approximately as in previous years.

1938 D &S   Low Mintage

Look at: 1938D and 1938S Jefferson Nickels.
Look for: These coins do not require any unique errors to contain a value. The low number of the coins minted gives a nice premium in any condition.
Mintage Numbers: 1938D   5,376,000   1938S   4,105,000

VALUE:

	Very Fine	Extra Fine	About Uncirculated	Uncirculated
1938D	1.00	1.75	2.50	4.00
1938S	2.00	2.75	3.50	4.25

1939 D &S Low Mintage

Look at: 1939D and 1939S Jefferson Nickels.
Look for: These coins do not require any unique errors to contain a value.
The low number of the coins minted gives a nice premium in any condition.
Mintage Numbers: 1939D   3,514,000   1939S   6,630,000

VALUE:

	Very Fine	Extra Fine	About Uncirculated	Uncirculated
1939D	1.00	1.75	2.50	4.00
1939S	2.00	2.75	3.50	4.25

1950 D Low Mintage

Look at: 1950 D Jefferson Nickels.
Look for: This coin does not require any unique errors to contain a value. The
low number of the 1950D minted gives a nice premium in any condition.
Mintage Numbers: 1950D   2,630,030

VALUE:

	Very Fine	Extra Fine	About Uncirculated	Uncirculated
1950D	5.00	5.25	5.50	6.50

Look at: MONTICELLO and FIVE CENTS on the Reverse.

Look for: A strong doubling on the right of all letters of MONTICELLO and FIVE CENT.

VALUE:

Extra Fine	About Uncirculated	Uncirculated
50.00	100.00	350.00

Listing Numbers
Breen#2665
Cherrypickers':FS-022
CONECA: DDR-001
Potter:VCR#1/DDR#1
Wexler: WDDR-001

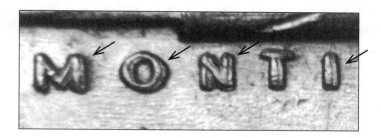

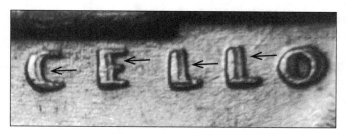

Very wide and bold doubling on the entire MONTICELLO.

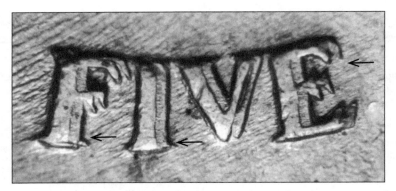

Notice notching and doubling on the letters of FIVE

Notice the strong doubling and heavy notching on the letters of CENTS

PHOTOS COURTESY OF: John Wexler

The 1939 Doubled Monticello variety is in high demand amongst collectors and can normally bring a very nice premium. Most dealers are aware of this highly publicized error.

If you have a coin in question, contact your local coin dealer for assistance.

WARNING: Strike Doubling is common on this date and should not be confused with the doubled dies shown here.

The Jefferson Nickel series is packed with a wide range of Doubled Obverses, Reverses, and many Doubled Mintmarks as well. Old nickels are common in pocket change and all warrant an examination.

Look at: OF AMERICA, UNITED STATES, and CENTS on the Reverse.
Look for: Strong doubling on the letters in OF AMERICA, UNITED STATES, and CENTS with strong notches on the bottoms of the letters.

VALUE:

Extra Fine	About Uncirculated	Uncirculated
15.00	25.00	50.00

Strong doubling of the letters in OF AMERICA on the reverse of the 1939 #2.

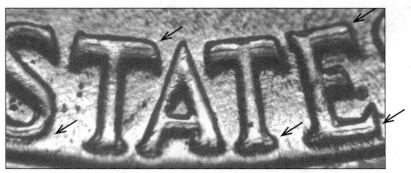

Equally strong doubling on the letters of UNITED STATES.

Listing Numbers
Potter: VCR#2/DDR#2
Wexler: WDDR-007

Look closely to detect the extra thick letters of FIVE CENTS.

PHOTOS COURTESY OF: John Wexler

Look at: S Mint mark near the bottom right of the building on the reverse.
Look for: A larger and much thicker S than the normal appearing S Mint Mark (see bottom photo).

VALUE:

Extra Fine	About Uncirculated	Uncirculated
10.00	20.00	50.00

This is the valuable and rare "Large S." Compare the size and shape to the normal S located in the photo below. There is very little magnification or skill required to spot the valuable variety.

Listing Numbers
Breen#-2676
Cherrypickers':FS-024.5
Potter:VCR#1/IMM#1

The is the "Normal S" that you will find on the majority of the 1941S Jefferson Nickels.

COIN COURTESY OF: Larry Briggs   *PHOTO COURTESY OF: Brian Allen*

1941-S   Inverted Mint Mark "up-side down S"

Look at: S Mint mark near the bottom right of the building on the reverse.
Look for: A small S Mint Mark with the "ball" portion of the main Mint Mark "upside-down."

VALUE:

Extra Fine	About Uncirculated	Uncirculated
25.00	50.00	150.00

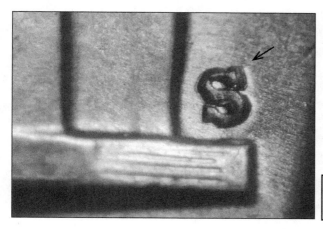

The arrow indicates the position of the "ball" on an upside down S. Compare to the photo below and you will notice the differences in the correctly intended orientation.

Listing Numbers
Cherrypickers':FS-024.6
Potter:VCR#1/IMM#1

A copy of this variety has sold for over $300!

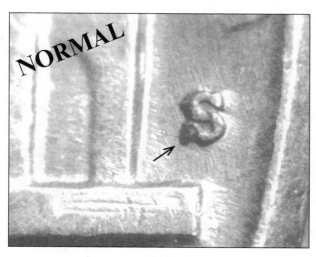

The arrow indicates the normal position of the "ball" portion of the S Mint Mark located on the bottom left of the S.

PHOTO COURTESY OF: Bill Fivaz

Look at: The number in the date and the front of Jefferson's nose.
Look for: A nice outline of the 2 in 1942 and doubling of Jefferson's nose.

VALUE:

Extra Fine	About Uncirculated	Uncirculated
55.00	85.00	150.00

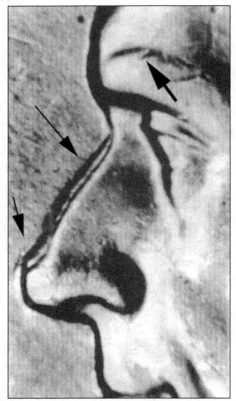

Listing Numbers
Cherrypickers':FS-025
CONECA: DDO-002
Potter:VCR#1/DDO#1
Wexler: WDDO-002

PHOTO COURTESY OF: John Wexler

Look at: The 42 in 1942 and the letters of TRUST

Look for: A strong notch on the vertical bar of the 4 and a strong doubled line on the outside upper curve of the 2.

VALUE:

Extra Fine	About Uncirculated	Uncirculated
35.00	65.00	125.00

Listing Numbers
Cherrypickers':FS-026
CONECA: DDO-003
Potter:VCR#2/DDO#2
Wexler: WDDO-001

The right upper portion of the 2 in 1942 with a portion of a second 2 protruding.

Very wide doubling of TRUST.

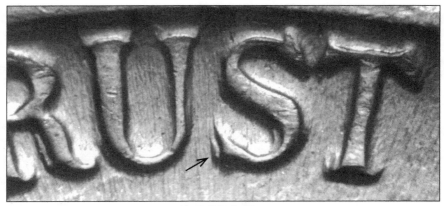

The RUST doubling.

A close up view of the doubled nose and lips on Jefferson's profile.

1942-D   Repunched Mint Mark "D/Horizontal D"

Look At: D on the reverse near the bottom right side of the building.
Look For: A strong horizontal bar in the middle and the lower loop of a horizontal D to the left side of the main D.

VALUE:

Extra Fine	About Uncirculated	Uncirculated
100.00	170.00	270.00

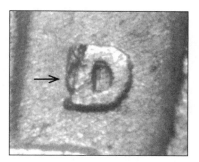

A strong horizontal repunched D is visible to the west and in the middle of the main D at the right base of MONTICELLO.

Listing Numbers
Breen#2681
Cherrypickers':FS-027
CONECA: RPM-001
Potter:VCR#1/RPM#1
Wexler: WRPM-001

COIN COURTESY OF: Brian Allen   *PHOTO COURTESY OF: Brian Allen*

1946-D   Repunched Mint Mark "D/Horizontal D"

Look At: D on the reverse of the coin.

Look For: A strong horizontal bar in the middle of the D Mint mark and the loop of the D protruding from the left.

VALUE:

Extra Fine	About Uncirculated	Uncirculated
125.00	200.00	400.00

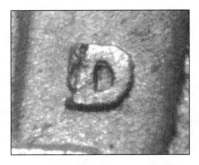

Listing Numbers
Breen#2708
Cherrypickers':FS-031
CONECA: RPM-002
Potter:VCR#1/RPM#1
Wexler: WRPM-002

COIN COURTESY OF: Brian Allen   *PHOTO COURTESY OF: Brian Allen*

Look at: LIBERTY and 1946 on the obverse.
Look for: Doubling to the west of the 1946 and LIBERTY.

VALUE:

Extra Fine	About Uncirculated	Uncirculated
65.00	100.00	275.00

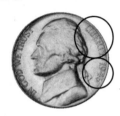

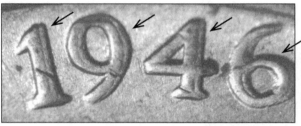

Strong lines to the right of all numbers of the date.

Listing Numbers
Breen#-2706
Cherrypickers':FS-031.5
CONECA: DDO-001
Potter:VCR#1/DDO#1
Wexler: WDDO-001

Not extremely wide but clearly visible separation on letters of LIBE.

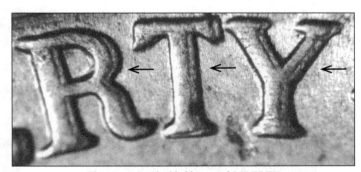

The remaining doubled letters of LIBERTY.

PHOTO COURTESY OF: John Wexler

Look At: D on the reverse of the coin near the right bottom of the MONTICELLO building.

Look For: A strong diagonal bar in the middle of the D Mint mark and the upper loop of the S protruding to the upper left.

VALUE:

Extra Fine	About Uncirculated	Uncirculated
55.00	100.00	300.00

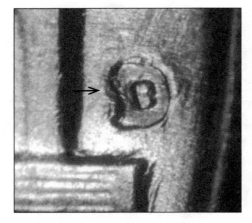

Portions of the underlying S are visible on top, to the left, and in the middle of the primary D at the right base of the MONTICELLO building on the reverse.

> **_Listing Numbers_**
> Breen#2720
> Cherrypickers':FS-032
> CONECA: OMM-001
> Potter:VCR#1/OMM#1
> Wexler: WOMM-001

COIN COURTESY OF: L&C Coin   *PHOTO COURTESY OF: Brian Allen*

Look at: E PLURIBUS UNUM on the Reverse.
Look for: Bold separation lines on the top and bottom of the lettering and very strong notches present at the tops and bottoms.

VALUE:

Extra Fine	About Uncirculated	Uncirculated
7.50	15.00	30.00

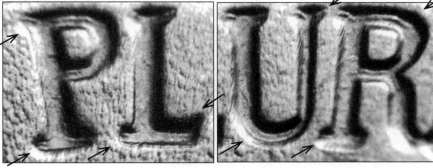

Easily noticed division lines on all letters of PLURIBUS.

The remainder of separation lines on PLURIBUS.

Listing Numbers
Wexler: WDDR-002

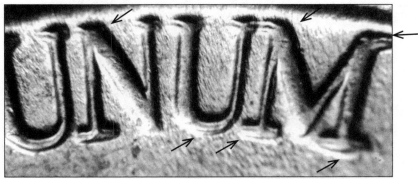

Very bold notches on the corners of UNUM with nice division lines.
PHOTO COURTESY OF: John Wexler

Look At: The D on the reverse of the coin near the bottom right side of the building.

Look For: A strong curve through the middle of the primary D Mint mark.

VALUE:

Extra Fine	About Uncirculated	Uncirculated
60.00	125.00	350.00

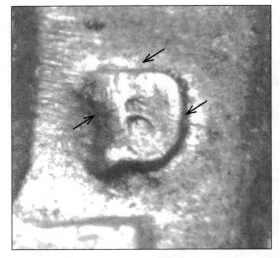

Some experts believe the underlying image to be that of a D, not an S. The coin will still command a nice premium regardless.

> **Listing Numbers**
> Breen#-2736
> Cherrypickers':FS-032.9
> CONECA: RPM-003
> Wexler: WOMM-001

PHOTO COURTESY OF: John Wexler

Look At: S on the reverse near the bottom right of the building.
Look For: A strong bar to the south of the S Mint mark and a vertical bar of a D in the loop of the S.

VALUE:

Extra Fine	About Uncirculated	Uncirculated
20.00	30.00	50.00

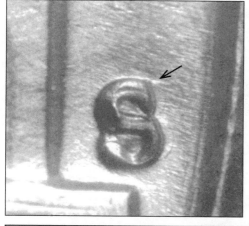

The D lies directly underneath of the S and is visible in the middle loop and to the south of the S. This is a very easy variety to detect and quite valuable.

Listing Numbers
Breen#-2734
Cherrypickers':FS-033
CONECA: OMM-001
Potter:VCR#1/OMM#1
Wexler: WOMM-001

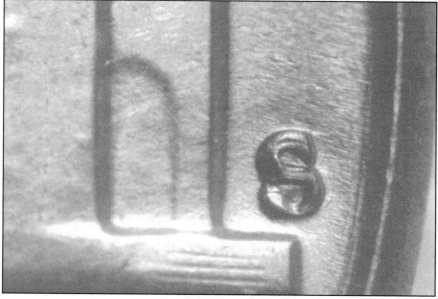

COIN COURTESY OF: Brian Allen   *PHOTO COURTESY OF: Brian Allen*

Look at: S Mint mark on the reverse near the bottom right of the building.
Look for: A nice second S to the north of the main S.

VALUE:

Extra Fine	About Uncirculated	Uncirculated
5.00	10.00	18.00

There are other 1954-S Jefferson Nickels with nicely doubled S's as well! Look closely at them all.

> **Listing Numbers**
> Cherrypickers':FS-033.1
> CONECA: RPM-001
> Potter:VCR#1/RPM#1
> Wexler: WRPM-001

COIN COURTESY OF: Frank Baumann   *PHOTO COURTESY OF: Brian Allen*

1955-D   Over Mint Mark "D over S #1"

Look at: The D Mint mark near the bottom right of the Monticello building, on the reverse of the coin.

Look for: A "D" over remnants of a fairly centered "S".

VALUE:

Extra Fine	About Uncirculated	Uncirculated
12.00	20.00	50.00

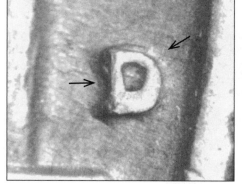

The "S" is visible in the middle loop of the "D" and to the top-left and top of the main "D" Mint mark.

> **_Listing Numbers_**
> Breen#-2739
> Cherrypickers':FS-034
> CONECA: OMM-001
> Potter:VCR#1/OMM#1
> Wexler: WOMM-001

COIN COURTESY OF: Brian Allen   *PHOTO COURTESY OF: Brian Allen*

Look at: The D Mint mark near the bottom right of the Monticello building on the reverse.

Look for: A protrusion on the top of the main D, with a diagonal line in the middle loop.

VALUE:

Extra Fine	About Uncirculated	Uncirculated
10.00	18.00	35.00

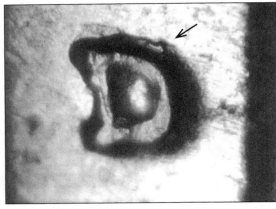

The underlying "S" is visible as a remnant to the Northeast and as a trace of the center loop within.

Listing Numbers
CONECA: OMM-002
Potter: VCR#2/OMM#2
Wexler: OMM-002

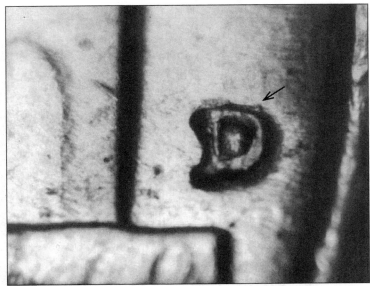

COIN COURTESY OF: Ken Potter   *PHOTO COURTESY OF: Ken Potter*

Look at: The D Mint mark near the bottom right of the Monticello building on the reverse.

Look for: A protrusion on the top of the main D, with a diagonal line in the middle loop and a protrusion to the east of the vertical bar.

VALUE:

Extra Fine	About Uncirculated	Uncirculated
3.75	6.00	15.00

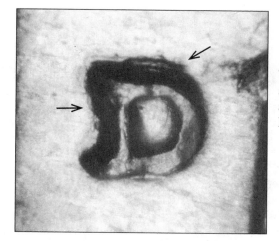

The underlying "S" is visible as a remnant to the Northeast and a as trace of the center loop within.

Listing Numbers
CONECA: OMM-003
Potter:VCR#3/OMM#3
Wexler: WOMM-003

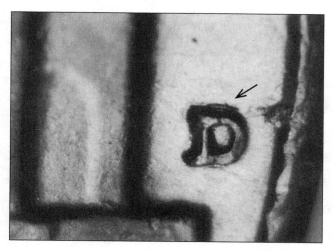

COIN COURTESY OF: Ken Potter

PHOTO COURTESY OF: Ken Potter

Look at: E PLURIBUS UNUM and UNITED STATES OF AMERICA on the reverse.

Look for: Very strong doubling of the letters and strong notches on the letters and division lines on tops of the letters.

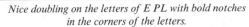

VALUE:

Extra Fine	About Uncirculated	Uncirculated
7.50	15.00	30.00

Listing Numbers
Wexler: WDDR-014

Nice doubling on the letters of E PL with bold notches in the corners of the letters.

The remaining letters of PLURIBUS with strong notches and doubling.

Very bold and wide doubling with notches on the letters of AMERICA.

The remaining letters of AMERICA.

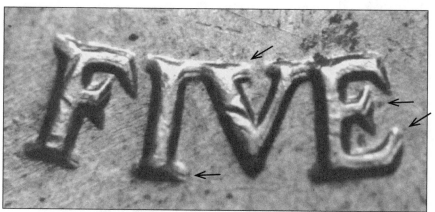

Not as bold on the letters of FIVE CENTS; however, there are strong notches on the letters to assist with identification.

PHOTO COURTESY OF: John Wexler

Look at: UNITED and E PLRIBUS UNUM on the Reverse.
Look for: Strong doubling of the letters with bold notches on the bottom of the letters.

VALUE:

Extra Fine	About Uncirculated	Uncirculated
7.50	15.00	30.00

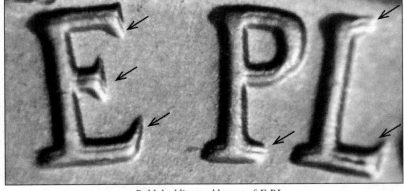

Bold doubling and letters of E PL.

The remaining letters of PLURIBUS.

Doubled lines on the letters of UNITED.

Listing Numbers
Wexler: WDDR-002

PHOTO COURTESY OF: John Wexler

Look at: UNITED and E PLURIBUS UNUM on the Reverse.
Look for: Strong doubling of the letters with bold notches in serifs.

VALUE:

Extra Fine	About Uncirculated	Uncirculated
7.50	15.00	30.00

Bold division lines on the tops and bottoms of the letters in E PLURIBUS.

Lesser doubling of "TATE".

<table>
<tr><td>Listing Numbers
Wexler: WDDR-041</td></tr>
</table>

PHOTO COURTESY OF: John Wexler

Doubled Mint Mark

Look at: The D near the bottom right of the Monticello.
Look for: A strong bar on the bottom right of the primary D and a portion of a secondary D in the gap between the Mint mark and the rim.

VALUE:

Extra Fine	About Uncirculated	Uncirculated
7.00	15.00	30.00

A very strong remnant of a second D is seen at the bottom right of the primary D.

Listing Numbers
CONECA: RPM-006
Potter:VCR#1/RPM#1
Wexler: WRPM-001

COIN COURTESY OF: Billy G. Crawford   *PHOTO COURTESY OF:* Billy G. Crawford

Doubled Die Reverse

Look at: UNITED STATES OF AMERICA on the Reverse.
Look for: Very strong doubling of the letters and there will be the strong notches on the letters.

VALUE:

Extra Fine	About Uncirculated	Uncirculated
7.50	15.00	30.00

Notice the very strong notches on the TE of UNITED.

Listing Numbers
Wexler: WDDR-008

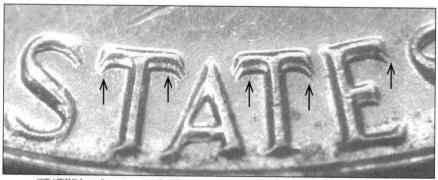

STATES has the strongest doubling present; again notice the notches along with the doubled letters. Notice the very strong notches on the TE of UNITED.

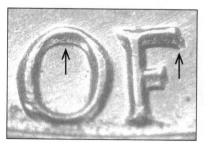 

The letters on OF are strongly doubled along with the CE of CENT.

COIN COURTESY OF: Larry Briggs   PHOTO COURTESY OF: Brian Allen

Look at: IN GOD WE TRUST, 2004 and the P Mint Mark.
Look for: Very strong doubling and notching on the letters.

VALUE:

Extra Fine	About Uncirculated	Uncirculated
50.00	125.00	300.00

NOTE: Prices listed here are for "early die states." Late to middle die states command under one-half of these prices listed. Contact a professional before selling or buying one of these varieties.

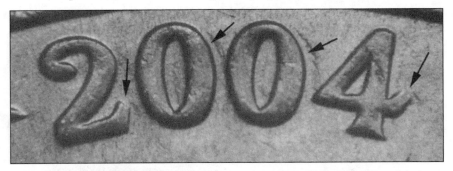

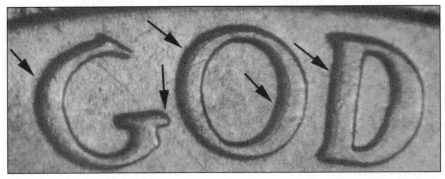

COIN COURTESY OF: BJ Neff   *PHOTO COURTESY OF: Brian Allen*

Listing Numbers
Cherrypickers':FS-05-2004P-101
CONECA: DDO-001
Potter:VCR#1/DDO#1
Wexler: WDDO-001

A FINAL WORD ON JEFFERSON NICKELS

The Jefferson Nickel series is packed with hundreds, possibly thousands, of varieties with new varieties being discovered frequently. The wide range of dates available for this series that you can pull from your pocket change makes discoveries possible for nearly every date. Look at all Jefferson Nickels dated 1964 and earlier and your chances of finding something significant will increase dramatically.

Many of the over 1,000 Doubled Dies and Repunched Mint Marks that are listed by the major attributers are minor and will bring very little as far as a premium. You are better off "saving" them up until you have a small number and then attempting to sell them as such. However the major and well-known varieties will normally sell quickly at a decent price.

The one difficulty with Jefferson Nickels is the often confusing deterioration or "contour" doubling that is visible on many coins. This type of doubling can be difficult to distinguish from a true hub doubling; however, once you have seen a few coins with die deterioration you will be able to quickly determine the difference.

Jefferson Nickels are true "sleepers" in the collecting hobby with a great many varieties hiding right in your pockets.

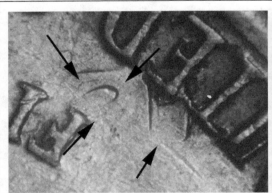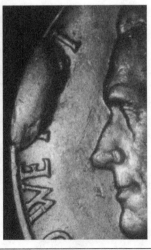

This 1983-P "CUD" shows the remnants of US of TRUST, remaining on the reverse die. This variety is valued between $150 - $300.

COIN COURTESY OF: GJ Lawson   *PHOTO COURTESY OF: Brian Allen*

Strike It Rich With Pocket Change

ROOSEVELT DIME VARIETIES

Composition: 90% silver and 10% copper
Years: 1946-1964
Weight: 2.50 Grams
Diameter: 17.9mm

Composition:75% copper and 25% nickel bonded to
a core of pure copper
Years: 1965-Current
Weight: 2.27 Grams
Diameter: 17.9mm

Mint Marked Years
Philadelphia 1946-Present
Denver 1946D-1964D, 68D-Present
San Francisco 1946S-1955S

Look at: 1965 Roosevelt dimes with a nice "silvery-white" appearance, look at the rim of the coin.

Look for: An edge that is uniform silver color. Additionally, if the coin is silver, it should weigh 2.5 grams (as opposed to the normal clad coin weight of 2.27 grams.)

VALUE:

Extra Fine	About Uncirculated	Uncirculated
2000.00	3800.00	5500.00

For a very easy "at-home" method of determining if your coin is the valuable silver transitional error or a normal coin turn to Chapter 11.

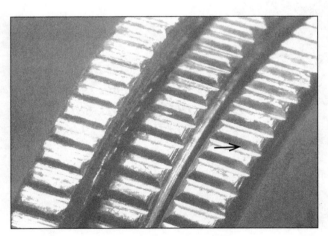

Listing Numbers
Breen#-3761

The two coins to the right are normal clad dimes.. Notice the two distinct colors of silver and reddish/brown. The coin on the left is a uniform color of silver. The coin on the left is the edge of a silver coin and the first clue that your 1965 could be the valuable transitional error.

Look at: 1966 Roosevelt dimes with a nice "silvery-white" appearance, look at the rim of the coin.

Look for: An edge that is uniform silver color. Additionally, if the coin is silver, it should weigh 2.5 grams (as opposed to the normal clad coin weight of 2.27 grams.)

VALUE:

Extra Fine	About Uncirculated	Uncirculated
2400.00	3800.00	5500.00

For a very easy "at-home" method of determining if your coin is the valuable silver transitional error or a normal coin turn to Chapter 11.

The two coins to the right are normal clad dimes.. Notice the two distinct colors of silver and reddish/brown. The coin on the left is a uniform color of silver. The coin on the left is the edge of a silver coin and the first clue that your 1965 could be the valuable transitional error.

Look at: The top of the torch and AMERICA on the reverse.
Look for: Strong notching on all flame tips and the upper left corners on the letters of AMERICA.

VALUE:

Extra Fine	About Uncirculated	Uncirculated
1.00	2.00	15.00

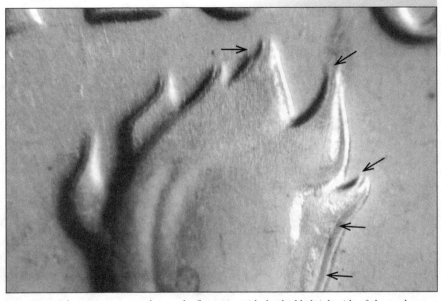

Notice the very strong notches on the flame tips with the doubled right side of the torch.

Notches on the upper portions of AMERICA

Listing Numbers
Potter:VCR#1/DDR#1
Wexler: WDDR-001

COIN COURTESY OF: Istavan Hendricks

PHOTO COURTESY OF: John Wexler

Look at: 1967 Roosevelt dimes with a nice "silvery-white" appearance, look at the rim of the coin.

Look for: An edge that is uniform silver color. Additionally, if the coin is silver, it should weigh 2.5 grams (as opposed to the normal clad coin weight of 2.27 grams.)

VALUE:

Extra Fine	About Uncirculated	Uncirculated
1800.00	2500.00	5500.00+

For a very easy "at-home" method of determining if you coin is the valuable silver transitional error or a normal coin turn to Chapter 11.

The two coins to the right are normal clad dimes.. Notice the two distinct colors of silver and reddish/brown. The coin on the left is a uniform color of silver. The coin on the left is the edge of a silver coin and the first clue that your 1965 could be the valuable transitional error.

Look at: the date, IN GOD WE TRUST and the JS.
Look for: Nice doubling on the upper loop of the 6; strong doubling on IN GOD and designer's initials; JS below Roosevelt's neck.

VALUE:

Extra Fine	About Uncirculated	Uncirculated
125.00	225.00	350.00

Listing Numbers
Breen#-3765
Cherrypickers':FS-019
CONECA: DDO-001
Potter:VCR#1/DDO#1
Wexler: WDDO-001

Very nice doubling seen on the 967 of the date

Very strong doubling seen on the GOD and TRUST

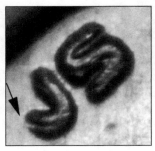

Very strong doubling seen on the designer's initials just below the neck line.

This doubled die is very rare with only a few copies known to exist!

PHOTOS COURTESY OF: JT Stanton

Look at: the 1968 and all letters of LIBERTY.
Look for: Bold doubling on 1968. Strong doubling on LIBERTY and JS.

VALUE:

Extra Fine	About Uncirculated	Uncirculated
45.00	85.00	175.00

Nice doubling on 968.

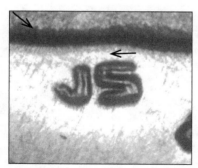

*The designer's initials JS (just below the neck)
shows very strong doubling*

Listing Numbers
CONECA: DDO-001
Potter:VCR#1/DDO#1
Wexler: WDDO-001

Easily detected doubling is evident on the right side of all letters of LIBERTY.

Nice doubling of ERTY of LIBERTY.

Traces of doubling evident on IN GOD WE TRUST.

COIN COURTESY OF: L&C Coin   *PHOTO COURTESY OF: Brian Allen*

Look at: The D above the date.
Look for: A very bold and wide Second D to the West.

VALUE:

Extra Fine	About Uncirculated	Uncirculated
25.00	50.00	75.00

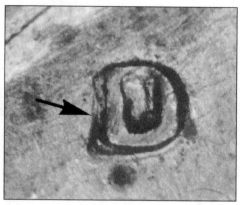

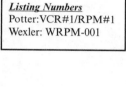

Listing Numbers
Potter:VCR#1/RPM#1
Wexler: WRPM-001

A strong secondary "D" shows west of the main "D."

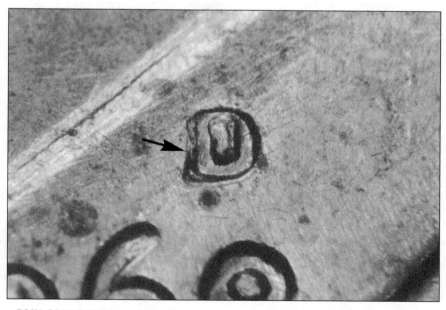

COIN COURTESY OF: John Bordner   *PHOTO COURTESY OF: John Bordner*

Look at: The D above the date.
Look for: A very bold and wide Second D to the East of the top D.

VALUE:

Extra Fine	About Uncirculated	Uncirculated
-	-	75.00- 125.00

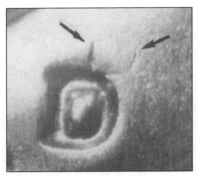

A very wide and visible D to the north of the main Mint mark.

Listing Numbers
CONECA: RPM-001
Potter:VCR#1/RPM#1
Wexler: WRPM-001

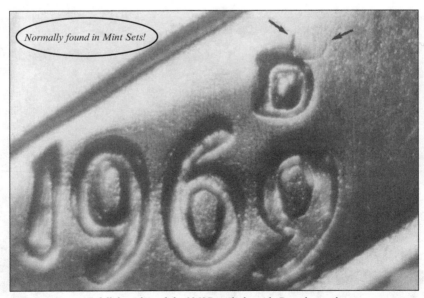

Normally found in Mint Sets!

A full date shot of the 1969D with the wide D to the north.

COIN COURTESY OF: H.M. Kuykendall   PHOTO COURTESY OF: Ken Potter

Look at: UNITED STATES OF AMERICA on the reverse.
Look for: Strong doubled letters and notching on the
letters in UNITED STATES OF AMERICA.

VALUE:

Extra Fine	About Uncirculated	Uncirculated
20.00	80.00	250.00

Look at the strongly doubled letters of STATES.

Listing Numbers
Breen#-3774
Cherrypickers':FS-020.6
CONECA: DDR-001
Potter:VCR#1/DDR#1
Wexler: WDDR-001

PHOTO COURTESY OF: John Wexler

Look At: The reverse lettering of UNITED STATES OF AMERICA.
Look For: Doubling on UNITED STATES, letters OF AMERICA;
strongest on AMERICA.

VALUE:

Extra Fine	About Uncirculated	Uncirculated
20.00	35.00	80.00

Slight doubling is visible on the bottoms of the letters of UNITED.

The doubling of STATES is slightly wider than that on UNITED.

Listing Numbers
CONECA: DDR-001
Potter:VCR#1/DDR#1
Wexler: WDDR-001

COIN COURTESY OF: Mike Ellis   *PHOTO COURTESY OF: Ken Potter*

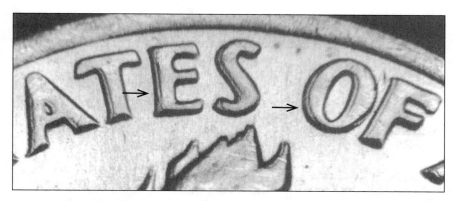

Doubling shows very well on OF UNITED STATES OF.

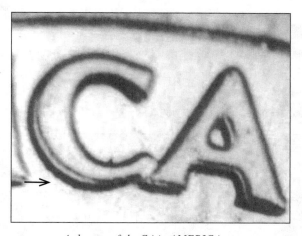

A close-up of the CA in AMERICA.

The strongest doubling is present on AMERICA.

Look At: OF AMERICA and UNUM on reverse.
Look For: Doubling on OF AMERICA, the last E in DIME and UNUM.

VALUE:

Extra Fine	About Uncirculated	Uncirculated
6.00	10.00	20.00

Bold lines to the left of the letters on OF in OF AMERICA.

Very distinct and clear doubling is shown on UNUM near the bottom of the torch and on the middle bar of the E in DIME.

Listing Numbers
CONECA: DDR-003 Potter:VCR#3/DDO#3   Wexler: WDDR-003

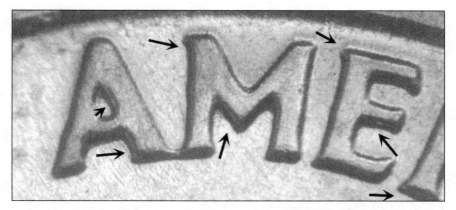

The doubling is not as strong on the inside portions of the AME of AMERICA; however, it is noticeable.

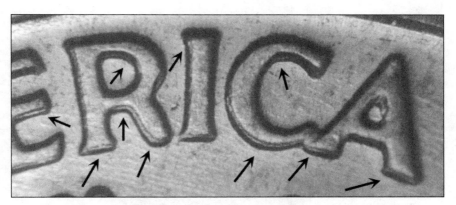

Much stronger doubling of RICA in AMERICA with the doubling showing on the bottom portions of the letters.

There are other nicely doubled Roosevelt dimes similar to the varieties shown in the last two listings. Most are not as apparent as these, but you may notice the doubling on coins in better condition. Coins of the early 1970s are a great place to start looking for nice Roosevelt dime varieties.

COIN COURTESY OF: *Frank Baumann*   PHOTO COURTESY OF: *Brian Allen*

Look at: The D Mint Mark below Roosevelt's neck.
Look for: A secondary D east of the main D.

VALUE:

Extra Fine	About Uncirculated	Uncirculated
12.00	18.00	35.00

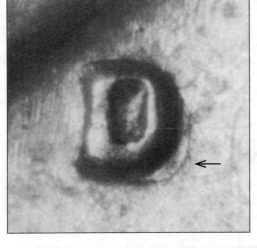

There are other 1971-D Repunched Mint Marks that are easily detected with low magnification.

> **Listing Numbers**
> Ken Potter:VCR#1/RPM#1
> Wexler: WRPM-001

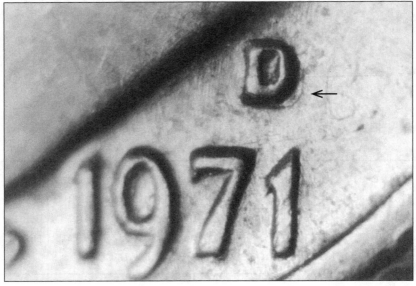

COIN COURTESY OF: H.M. Kuykendall   *PHOTO COURTESY OF: Ken Potter*

Look at: The upper neckline just above the P Mint mark.
Look for: The vertical bar of a "P" is visible well above the main "P" just below the neck.

VALUE:

Extra Fine	About Uncirculated	Uncirculated
25.00	50.00	150.00

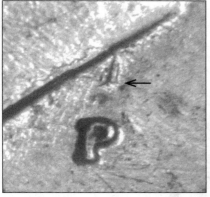

The bottom portion of a misplaced P Mint Mark is visible below Roosevelt's Neck.

> **Listing Numbers**
> Potter:VCR#1/RPM#1
> Wexler: WRPM-001

A large view of the date and misplace Mint Mark location.

PHOTO COURTESY OF: John Wexler

Look at: Area above the date, just below the neck.
Look for: The absence of a P. (These were struck in Philadelphia.)

VALUE:

Extra Fine	About Uncirculated	Uncirculated
20.00	30.00	75.00

Listing Numbers
Breen#-3816
Cherrypickers':FS-021
Potter:VCR#1/MMO#1

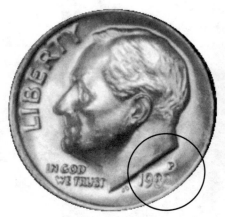

This is a shot of a normal 1982-P Roosevelt dime with the P Mint mark in the proper location. Photo Courtesy of: Brian Allen

A comparison photo of a 1982 with missing Mint mark.

COIN COURTESY OF: *Abbott's*

PHOTO COURTESY OF: *Ken Potter*

Look at: IN GOD WE TRUST.

Look for: A misplaced horizontal D punched between the US of TRUST.

VALUE:

Extra Fine	About Uncirculated	Uncirculated
25.00	50.00	150.00

A nice upside D visible below the US of TRUST.

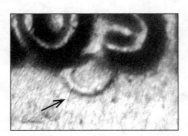

A close up shot of the Horizontal D below TRUST.

Listing Numbers
Potter: VCR#1/RPM#1   Wexler: WRPM-001

PHOTO COURTESY OF: John Wexler

Look at: The D above the date.
Look for: A very strong second D to the North of the primary D.

VALUE:

Extra Fine	About Uncirculated	Uncirculated
10.00	15.00	30.00

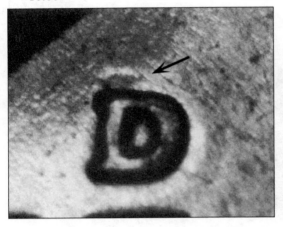

Listing Numbers
Potter:VCR#1/RPM#1
Wexler: WRPM-001

A strong portion of a second D that is protruding from the top of the main D.

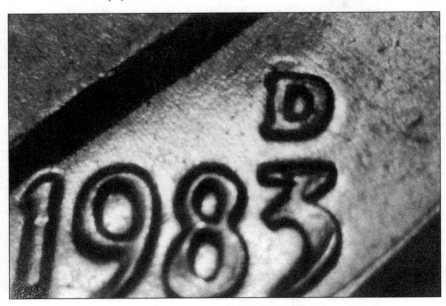

PHOTO COURTESY OF: John Wexler

Look at: D above the date.

Look for: A strong secondary "D" to the south of the primary "D."

VALUE:

Extra Fine	About Uncirculated	Uncirculated
10.00	20.00	30.00

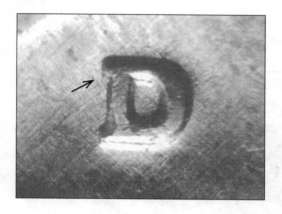

> **Listing Numbers**
> Potter: VCR#2/RPM#2
> Wexler: WRPM-002

A full date view with the repunched D to the south of the primary D.

COIN COURTESY OF: Richard Imbaguria   *PHOTO COURTESY OF: John Bordner*

Look at: D above the date.
Look for: A strong secondary "D" to the south of the primary "D."

VALUE:

Extra Fine	About Uncirculated	Uncirculated
10.00	20.00	30.00

> **_Listing Numbers_**
> Potter:VCR#3/RPM#3
> Wexler: WRPM-003

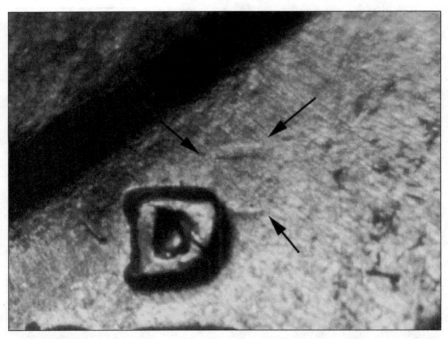

Remnant of a Horizontal "D" is visible directly above and to the right of the main "D."

PHOTO COURTESY OF: John Wexler

Look at: The back of the neck behind the ear.
Look for: An outlined shape of a P struck on the neck of Roosevelt.

VALUE:

Extra Fine	About Uncirculated	Uncirculated
35.00	60.00	150.00

> **Listing Numbers**
> Wexler: WRPM-001

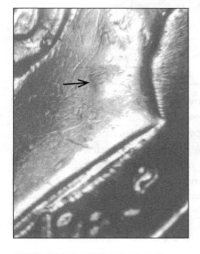

What appears to be the outline of a P stamped into the neckline is visible below and just behind the ear on Roosevelt's head.

The exact nature of this variety is in dispute amongst specialists. Some believe it's classification is unproven or that it is the result of less significant causes. Nonetheless, it still commands a significant premium amongst proponents of the variety.

COIN COURTESY OF: Mark Longas   PHOTO COURTESY OF: Ken Potter

1986-P

Look at: The area just above the P Mint mark.
Look for: An outlined shape of a P struck next to the rim above the normal P.

VALUE:

Extra Fine	About Uncirculated	Uncirculated
35.00	60.00	150.00

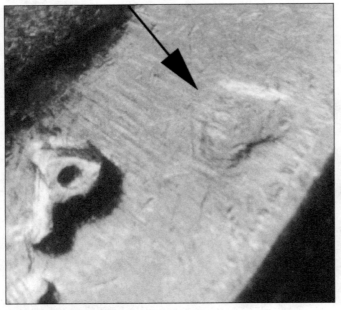

Listing Numbers
Wexler: WRPM-001

The exact nature of this variety is in dispute amongst specialist. Some believe it's classification is unproven or that it is the result of less significant causes. None the less, it still commands a significant premium amongst proponents of the variety.

COIN COURTESY OF: Richard Carlson   *PHOTO COURTESY OF: John Bordner*

Look at: The D directly above the date.
Look for: A repunched D north of the primary D.

VALUE:

Extra Fine	About Uncirculated	Uncirculated
8.00	12.00	25.00

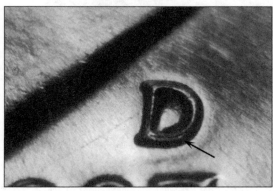

Listing Numbers
CONECA: RPM-001
Potter:VCR#1/RPM#1
Wexler: WRPM-001

COIN COURTESY OF: Brian Allen   *PHOTO COURTESY OF: Brian Allen*

ABOUT ROOSEVELT DIMES

In comparison to other denominations, the Roosevelt dime series has fewer varieties; however, they are highly collected and carry nice premiums. The area of Roosevelt dimes is beginning to grow as collectors find numerous new errors each year drawing much needed attention to the Roosevelt dime series.

A good example of the rarity on Roosevelt dimes is the Rotated Reverse Errors, for which there are no known examples. This would lead anyone to believe that a discovery of a Rotated Reverse Roosevelt Dime would be extremely rare and valuable, but most of all easy to detect to the non-coin collector. If you are looking to find coins that will quickly sell at a nice price, Roosevelt dimes could be your answer.

A DREAM COME TRUE.............
This would surely make your day! This is a 2000-P Massachusetts Quarter that was struck a second time by a 2000-P Sacagawea dollar! This type of error can bring significant values often in the thousands of dollars.

More great 50 States Quarter Errors later in the book!

Coin and photo courtesy of Abbott's Coin Exchange. Birmingham, Michigan

WASHINGTON QUARTER VARIETIES

Composition: 90% silver and 10% copper
Years: 1932-1964
Weight: 6.25 Grams
Diameter: 24.3mm

Composition: Outer layers of copper-nickel
copper 75% and nickel 25%
bonded to a core of pure copper.
Years: 1965-Present
Weight: 5.75 Grams
Diameter: 24.3mm

Mint Marked Years
Philadelphia 1965-Present
Denver 1968D-Present

Look at: The thickness of the edge and very weak or poorly defined features.
Look for: Very weak details and a Quarter that is the thickness of a Roosevelt dime with very few detailed reeds on the coin's edge.

VALUE:

Extra Fine	About Uncirculated	Uncirculated
10.00	30.00	75.00

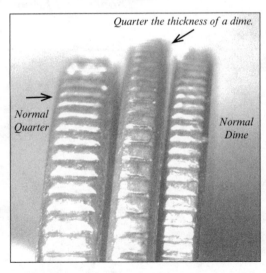

Quarter the thickness of a dime.

Normal Quarter

Normal Dime

IT IS POSSIBLE TO FIND THIS TYPE OF ERROR ON MANY OTHER DATES!

The coin on the far left is the rim of a normal Washington Quarter, the middle coin is the Quarter struck on a dime thin planchet while the far right is a normal dime.

Note the lack of rim reeds on the middle quarter from lack of pressure during the strike.

This error is rather easy to pick up just because of the very light weight of the coin and the poor features. This is possible on any denomination especially 5c, 10c and 25c because all of the metals look the same and are sometimes confused. This is known to have occurred on nearly all coins but the 1970D 25c is very prominent for the mint apparently did not catch the mistake and several hundreds to thousands were made. The dime thick quarter should weigh between 4.2 and 4.4 grams. The weight can vary greatly so look at all the details and thickness. While looking at quarters that are rolled in plastic you may pick up coins that appear very thin, start there!

COIN COURTESY OF: Brian Allen   *PHOTO COURTESY OF: Brian Allen*

Look at: IN GOD WE TRUST and the letters of LIBERTY.
Look for: Very bold doubled letters on IN GOD WE TRUST and moderate doubling on the letters of LIBERTY.

VALUE:

Extra Fine	About Uncirculated	Uncirculated
500.00	1000.00	2000.00

Very bold doubling on IN GOD WE TRUST makes this coin easily identified.

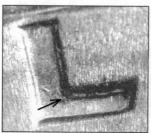  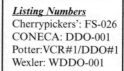

> **Listing Numbers**
> Cherrypickers': FS-026
> CONECA: DDO-001
> Potter:VCR#1/DDO#1
> Wexler: WDDO-001

Nice doubling is seen on all the letters of LIBERTY.

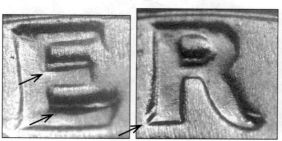 

COIN COURTESY OF: L&C Coin/Pete Goydos   PHOTO COURTESY OF: Brian Allen

Look at: 1965 Quarters with a shiny finish and a uniform colored rim.

Look for: The weight will be slightly heavier at 6.25 grams in comparison to a normal quarter weighing 5.67 grams. The Silver quarter is slightly thicker on the edge.

VALUE:

Extra Fine	About Uncirculated	Uncirculated
2500.00	3500.00	5000.00

For a very easy "at-home" method of determining if your coin is the valuable silver transitional error or a normal coin, turn to Chapter 11.

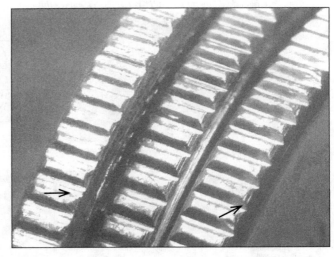

Notice the solid silver appearance.

The two coin rims on the right are of a normal clad quarter. Notice the "sandwich" color of silver and a reddish/brown layer. The coin on the left is a uniform color of silver. This is the rim of a silver coin and the first clue that your 1965 is the valuable transitional error.

PHOTO COURTESY OF: Brian Allen

Look at: UNITED STATES OF AMERICA and QUARTER DOLLAR on the reverse.

Look for: Moderately strong doubled lines on the letters of UNITED, AMERICA and on the letters of QUARTER.

VALUE:

Extra Fine	About Uncirculated	Uncirculated
250.00	400.00	1000.00

> **Listing Numbers**
> Cherrypickers':FS-06.3
> CONECA: DDR-001
> Potter:VCR#1/DDR#1
> Wexler: WDDR-001

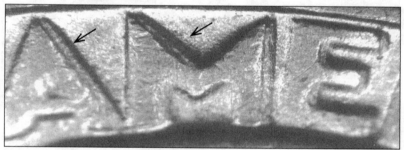

Evenly doubled letters on AMERICA on the reverse; notice the strong lines on the right side of the letters.

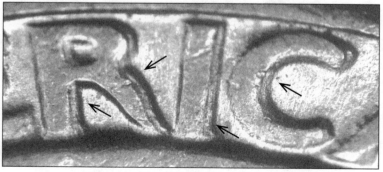

Close-up of the doubled RICA of AMERICA.

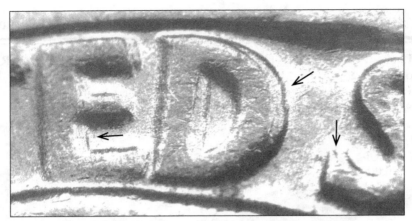

A close up of the ED S of the last two letters of UNITED and the first S of STATES. Very bold on the inside and out of the D.

The lettering on the left side of QUARTERS is doubled as well, although not as heavily as AMERICA.

Close-up shot of the AR in QUARTER.

COIN COURTESY OF: L&C Coin/Pete Goydos   PHOTO COURTESY OF: Brian Allen

Strike It Rich With Pocket Change

Look at: UNITED STATES OF AMERICA on the reverse.
Look for: Boldly doubled letters on the entire reverse.

VALUE:

Extra Fine	About Uncirculated	Uncirculated
2.00	375.00	750.00

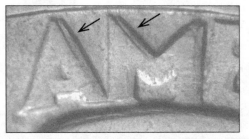

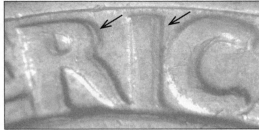

Here we see the strong doubling that is shifted to the right side of the letters in AMERICA.

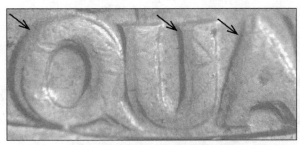

The strong doubling of QUA on QUARTER.

Listing Numbers
Potter:VCR#1/DDR#1
Wexler: WDDR-001

Strong bars on all letters of DOLLAR.

Light doubling on UNITED is best seen on the bottom right bars of the IT and the insides of the E and D of UNITED. Notice the strong lines visible on the ends of the E.

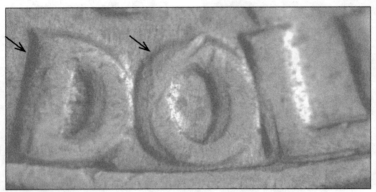

DOLLAR has very thick letters with nice division lines visible.

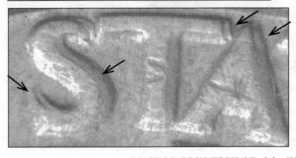

STA of STATES is strongly doubled on all portions of the lettering.

Strike It Rich With Pocket Change

Look at: The D Mint Mark behind Washington's head on 1969-D Quarters.
Look for: A small portion of a second D protruding from the left of the primary D Mint Mark.

VALUE:

Extra Fine	About Uncirculated	Uncirculated
8.00	10.00	20.00

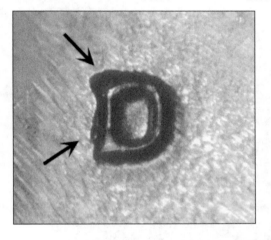

Listing Numbers
CONECA: RPM-001
Potter:VCR#1/RPM#1
Wexler: WRPM-001

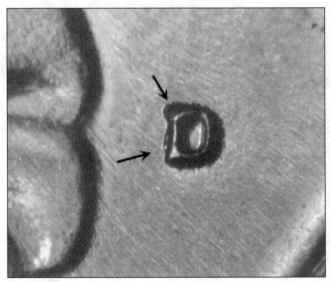

COIN COURTESY OF: Frank Baumann   PHOTO COURTESY OF: Brian Allen

Look at: The 1970 and IN GOD WE TRUST.
Look for: Very strong doubling on the 1 of the date, doubling on 970 and on IN GOD WE TRUST.

VALUE:

Extra Fine	About Uncirculated	Uncirculated
500.00	750.00	1250.00

Very significant doubling is noticeable on all the letters of IN GOD WE TRUST.

Listing Numbers
Cherrypickers':FS-027.3
CONECA: DDO-001
Potter:VCR#1/DDO#1
Wexler: WDDO-001

*Look at the upper left and lower right corner of the 1 and you can see the strong
notches along with a strong division line on the left side of the 1.
The 9 has very evident doubling on the bottom portion of the loop.*

*Much like the 19 of the date, the 7 presents us with nice notches on the upper left
and lower right corners and has a strong division line on the left of the bar.
The 0 has a strong division line on the lower left loop.*

COIN COURTESY OF: *Jim Lafferty*   PHOTO COURTESY OF: *Kevin Flynn*

**Updated prices for coins listed in this book can be seen at
our web-site: http://koinpro.tripod.com/Treasures.htm**

Look at: UNITED STATES OF AMERICA and QUARTER DOLLAR on the reverse.

Look for: Very thick letters of UNITED STATES with visible separation lines.

VALUE:

Extra Fine	About Uncirculated	Uncirculated
750.00	1000.00	1500.00

Listing Numbers	
Cherrypickers': FS-027.7	CONECA: DDR-001
Potter:VCR#1/DDR#1	
Wexler: WDDR-001	

Very nice doubling on all letters of QUARTER.

Strong notching and doubling is evident on DOLLAR.

UNITED has very bold doubling present on all letters.

1971 Doubled Die Reverse Cont.

A close-up of the UNI of UNITED. You can see the notching in the lower left corners and the strong separation lines.

A close-up of the TED of UNITED. Notice the strong lines on the T and on the inside of the E and D with a nice doubled outside loop of the D.

A close-up of the STA of STATES. You can see very heavy notches on the right bar of the T and lower legs of the A. Also strong doubled line on all letters and a nice doubled loop on the outside of the S.

PHOTO COURTESY OF: John Wexler

Look at: STATES OF AMERICA on reverse.

Look for: Very thick letters with separation lines present on the letters of STATES OF AMERICA.

VALUE:

Extra Fine	About Uncirculated	Uncirculated
250.00	400.00	650.00

Listing Numbers

Cherrypickers':FS-027.8   CONECA: DDR-001

Potter:VCR#1/DDR#1

Wexler: WDDR-001

The photo above and below shows the lines on the left of the letters in AMERICA

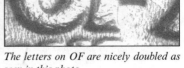

Very easily seen on the T's and A of STATES on the left side of the letters.

The letters on OF are nicely doubled as seen in this photo.

COIN COURTESY OF: L&C Coin/Pete Goydos

PHOTO COURTESY OF: Brian Allen

Doubled Die Obverse

Look at: The letters of LIBERTY and the IN of IN GOD WE TRUST.
Look for: Strong doubling on all letters of LIBERTY and upper corners of IN GOD.

VALUE:

Extra Fine	About Uncirculated	Uncirculated
350.00	800.00	1500.00

Strong separation on LIBERTY.

A closer view of the doubling on the letters of LIBERTY.

The doubling on this coin may be difficult to detect in well circulated coins. Examine the entire coin thoroughly.

Each letter of LIBERTY has nice notching on the top and the strong bars on the left side.

Listing Numbers
Breen#4452
Cherrypickers':FS-028v
CONECA: DDO-001
Potter:VCR#1/DDO#1
Wexler: WDDO-001

A close-up of the BE in LIBERTY.

A close-up of the doubling on the RT of LIBERTY.

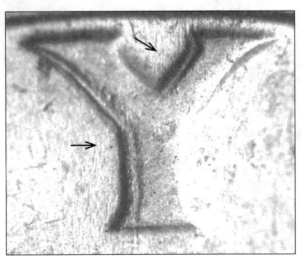

Close-up of the Y in LIBERTY.

Keep an eye out for these strong lines on the left side of the letters.

COIN COURTESY OF: *Ron Pope*

PHOTO COURTESY OF: *Kevin Flynn*

Strike It Rich With Pocket Change

Look at: The D behind the head.
Look for: A strong vertical bar of a secondary D east of the primary D.

VALUE:

Extra Fine	About Uncirculated	Uncirculated
5.00	10.00	20.00

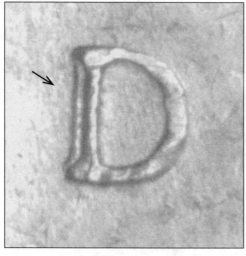

A strong secondary bar to the left side of the primary D Mint Mark

Listing Numbers
CONECA: RPM-001
Potter:VCR#1/RPM#1
Wexler: WRPM-001

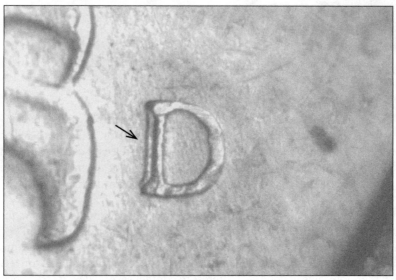

COIN COURTESY OF: *H.M. Kuykendall*   PHOTO COURTESY OF: *Ken Potter*

Look at: Delaware, Pennsylvania, New Jersey and Connecticut Quarters.
Look for: Circulated or Uncirculated Coins

VALUE:

State	About Uncirculated	Uncirculated
Delaware P	1.00	2.00
Delaware D	1.50	2.25
Pennsylvania P	1.00	2.00
Pennsylvania D	1.50	2.25
New Jersey P	0.50	1.25
New Jersey D	0.75	1.50
Connecticut P	0.50	1.25
Connecticut D	0.50	1.00

There was no way of knowing the impact that the new 50 States Quarter Program would have on the general public or the coin collector. The states listed above where not "hoarded" in mass like the subsequent releases causing a shortage which has driven up the price dramatically. This is one of the most prolific jumps for a normal circulation coin during the first year of any modern release.

These coins can be sold for a small premium in circulated condition, just as you would find them in circulation. The prices listed above are "retail" prices as if you were to purchase a copy, you should expect to get a smaller amount if you are attempting to sell. The market value of coins can change on a daily basis; therefore, it is in your best interest to contact several dealers to determine the best location to sell.

Rotated Reverse

Look at: All Washington Quarters.

Look for: See the details listed on the bottom of this page.

VALUE: *For 90-180 degree rotations.*

Extra Fine	About Uncirculated	Uncirculated
55.00	125.00	300.00

CIRCULATION WASHINGTON QUARTER DATES
WITH KNOWN ROTATIONS

1965

1966

1972-D

1985

1989-P

1999-P & D *(All five states issued for 1999)*

For further details on how to determine Rotated Reverse look in the chapter on Errors.

JOHN F. KENNEDY HALF-DOLLAR VARIETIES

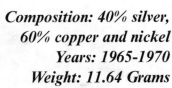

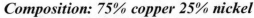

Composition: silver 90% and copper 10%
Years: 1964
Weight: 12.5 Grams
Diameter: 30.6mm

Composition: 40% silver,
60% copper and nickel
Years: 1965-1970
Weight: 11.64 Grams
Diameter: 30.6mm

Composition: 75% copper 25% nickel
Years: 1971-Present
Weight: 11.50 Grams
Diameter: 30.6mm

Mint Mark Years
Philadelphia 1964-Present
Denver 1964D, 68D-Present
San Francisco No circulation releases

1971-D On a Silver Blank

Look at: 1971D Kennedy Half-Dollars.
Look for: A brilliant, shiny coin that weighs 11.50 grams.

VALUE:

Extra Fine	About Uncirculated	Uncirculated
750.00	1500.00	2500.00

Due to the rarities in locating a true 1977D JF Kennedy on a silver clad planchet, the above photo is of a normal clad issue Kennedy Half-Dollar.

This variety will be difficult to locate, but well worth the effort. There are few describable features to clue in on the small fortune. A suspect coin may have a shiny reflective finish, much like silver coinage. The first step to helping you with identifying this coin is to use the "tissue-overlay" method shown in Chapter 9. Because the Kennedy Half-Dollars or the Eisenhower Dollar coins only contain 20 & 40% silver, you will not be able to determine the silver content by looking for the sandwich colors on the edge of the rim (as shown in the Dime and Quarter section). You will need to use all available options to help you with this coin.

The second step to identify the variety is to weigh the coin. The weight of the silver-clad error will be 11.50 grams and the clad coinage will weigh 11.34 grams. The difference is very minor and could be misleading. The only true method of determination is by performing a specific gravity test to determine the metal composition. This test, although not extremely complicated, is time consuming.

PHOTO COURTESY OF: Brian Allen

Look at: IN GOD WE TRUST on the obverse.
Look for: Strong doubling on TRUST, and notches on IN GOD WE and LIBERTY.

VALUE:

Extra Fine	About Uncirculated	Uncirculated
8.00	15.00	40.00

Notice the very strong lines that are present on all letters of TRUST.

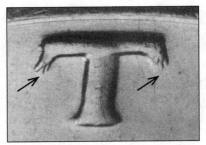

Very strong notches are visible on serifs at the upper bar of the T in LIBERTY; doubling is also present on vertical bar.

Listing Numbers
CONECA: DDO-001
Potter:VCR#1/DDO#1
Wexler: WDDO-001

Very strong notches are seen on the corners of the I in IN GOD WE TRUST.

COIN COURTESY OF: Ken Potter   *PHOTO COURTESY OF: Ken Potter*

Look at: IN GOD WE TRUST on the obverse.
Look for: Strong doubling on TRUST, very strong on the R of TRUST and notches on IN GOD WE.

VALUE:

Extra Fine	About Uncirculated	Uncirculated
25.00	40.00	75.00

The doubling is most evident on WE TRUST.

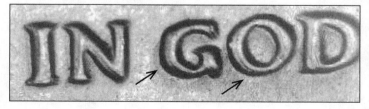

Nice doubling is visible on IN GOD.

Listing Numbers

CONECA: DDO-001	Potter:VCR#1/DDO#1	Wexler: WDDO-001

COIN COURTESY OF: Peter Beane & Jennifer Casazza PHOTO COURTESY OF: Ken Potter

1972-D No FG

Look at: The small gap between the eagle's left leg and the tail feathers on the reverse.
Look for: The absence of the FG under the right arm.

VALUE:

Extra Fine	About Uncirculated	Uncirculated
4.00	8.00	10.00

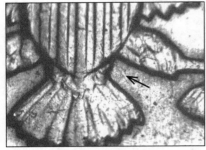

No FG under the right leg.

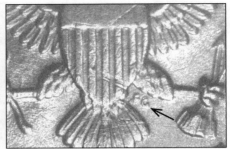

Normal coin with FG present.

1973-D No F

Look at: The small gap between the eagle's left leg and the tail feathers on the reverse.
Look for: Small remains of the G and no F of FG.

VALUE:

Extra Fine	About Uncirculated	Uncirculated
3.00	5.00	10.00

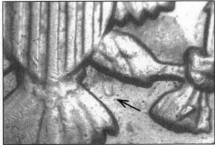

No F under the right leg with only G remaining.

Normal coin with FG present.

It is possible to find the No F and No FG on any date of the Half Dollar. Look at all dates even those not listed here and you may find a new discovery.

COIN COURTESY OF: Ken Potter   *PHOTO COURTESY OF: Ken Potter*

1973-D   Doubled Die Obverse

Look at: TRUST of IN GOD WE TRUST.
Look for: Strong doubling of TRUST and slightly
on the upper loop of the 3 of the date.

VALUE:

Extra Fine	About Uncirculated	Uncirculated
50.00	75.00	150.00

Listing Numbers
Cherrypickers':FS-014.8
CONECA: DDO-002
Potter:VCR#1/DDO#1
Wexler: WDDO-002

COIN COURTESY OF: Ken Potter   *PHOTO COURTESY OF: Ken Potter*

1973-D   Repunched Mint Mark

Look at: The D Mint mark below the Neck on the obverse.
Look for: A strong second D to the north of the primary D.

VALUE:

Extra Fine	About Uncirculated	Uncirculated
5.00	7.00	15.00

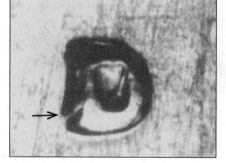

*A very strong doubled Mint mark is visible
on the left side of the main D.*

Listing Numbers
CONECA: RPM-001
Potter:VCR#2/RPM#1
Wexler: WRPM-001

PHOTO COURTESY OF: John Wexler

Look at: IN GOD WE TRUST on the obverse.
Look for: Very strong doubling on TRUST and notching on IN GOD WE and LIBERTY.

VALUE:

Extra Fine	About Uncirculated	Uncirculated
20.00	35.00	75.00 - 100.00

Listing Numbers
Breen#5299
CONECA: DDO-001
Cherrypickers':FS-015
Potter:VCR#1/DDO#1
Wexler: WDDO-001

Very bold doubling on IN GOD WE TRUST

Keep your eyes open on all JFK Half-Dollars, there are dozens of doubled obverses. Most of the others are considered minor and do not have the same value but are nice finds worth looking for.

COIN COURTESY OF: Ken Potter　　　　*PHOTO COURTESY OF: Ken Potter*

Look at: 1977D Kennedy Half Dollars.

Look for: A brilliant, silvery appearance and a weight of 11.50 grams.

VALUE:

Extra Fine	About Uncirculated	Uncirculated
1000.00	2000.00	3500.00

Due to the difficulty in locating a true 1977D JF Kennedy on a silver clad planchet, the above photo is of a normal clad issue Kennedy Half-Dollar.

This variety will be difficult to locate, but well worth the effort if found. There are few describable features to clue in on the small fortune. A suspect coin may have a shiny reflective finish, much like silver coinage. The first step to helping you with identifying this coin is to use the "tissue-overlay" method shown in Chapter 9. Because the Kennedy Half-Dollars or the Eisenhower Dollar coins only contain 20 & 40% silver you will not be able to determine the silver content by looking for the sandwich colors on the edge of the rim (as shown in the Dime and Quarter section). You will need to use all available options to help you with this coin.

The second step to identify the variety is to weigh the coin. The weight of the silver-clad error will be 11.50 grams and the clad coinage will weigh 11.34 grams. The difference is very minor and could be misleading. The only true method of determination is by performing a specific gravity test to determine the metal composition. This test, although not extremely complicated, is time consuming.

PHOTO COURTESY OF: Brian Allen

1977-D

Look at: The area between the eagle's left leg and the tail feathers on the reverse.
Look for: Partial G and no F of FG.

VALUE:

Extra Fine	About Uncirculated	Uncirculated
3.75	6.00	15.00

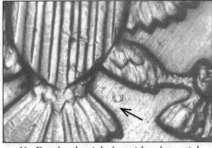

No F under the right leg with only partial G remaining

COIN COURTESY OF: Ken Potter

PHOTO COURTESY OF: Ken Potter

1982-P

No FG

Look at: The area between the eagle's left leg and the tail feathers on the reverse.
Look for: FG missing where it is normally located.

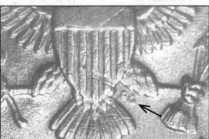

VALUE:

Extra Fine	About Uncirculated	Uncirculated
3.75	6.00	15.00

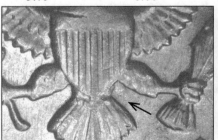

No FG under the right leg.

COIN COURTESY OF: Frank Baumann

PHOTO COURTESY OF: Brian Allen

1983-P No FG

Look at: The area between the eagle's left leg and the tail feathers on the reverse.
Look for: FG missing where it is normally located.

VALUE:

Extra Fine	About Uncirculated	Uncirculated
3.25	5.00	10.00

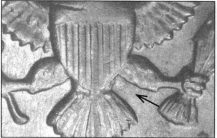

No FG under the right leg.

COIN COURTESY OF: Frank Baumann

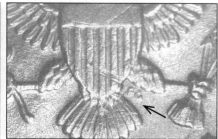

Normal coin with FG present.

PHOTO COURTESY OF: Brian Allen

1989-P No FG

Look at: The area between the eagles left leg and the tail feathers on the reverse.
Look for: FG missing where it is normally located.

VALUE:

Extra Fine	About Uncirculated	Uncirculated
3.75	6.00	15.00

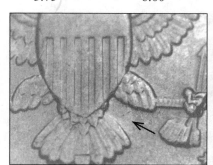

No FG under the right leg.

COIN COURTESY OF: Ken Potter

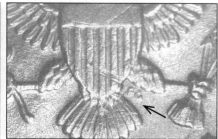

Normal coin with FG present.

PHOTO COURTESY OF: Ken Potter

Look at: The D Mint Mark below Kennedy's neckline on 1989-D Half-Dollar.
Look for: A small portion of a second D protruding from the top left
portion of the primary D Mint Mark.

VALUE:

Extra Fine	About Uncirculated	Uncirculated
8.00	10.00	20.00

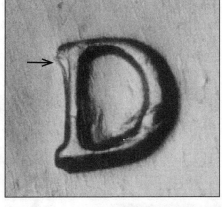

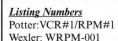

*A portion of the secondary D Mint Mark
is seen protruding from the top left corner
of the main D Mint Mark and slightly
visible on the bottom bar.*

> **Listing Numbers**
> Potter:VCR#1/RPM#1
> Wexler: WRPM-001

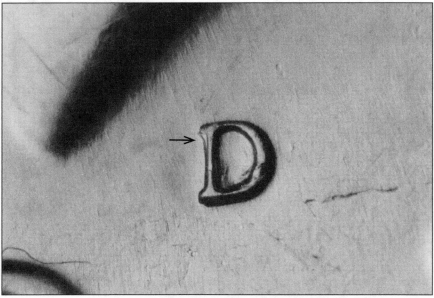

PHOTO COURTESY OF: Ken Potter

EISENHOWER/SUSAN B ANTHONY DOLLAR VARIETIES

Composition: silver 40% bonded to core of pure copper
Years: 1971S, 1972S, 1973S, 1974S, 1976S
Weight: 24.59 Grams
Diameter: 38.1mm

Composition: 75% copper 25% nickel
Years: 1971PD-1976PD and
1977 & 1978 PDS
Weight: 22.68 Grams
Diameter: 38.1mm

Mint Marked Years
Philadelphia 1971-1978
Denver 1971D-1978D
San Francisco 1971S-1978S

SUSAN B ANTHONY DOLLARS
Composition: 75% copper, 25% nickel
Years: 1979-81, 1999
Weight: 8.1 Grams
Diameter: 26.5mm

SACAGAWEA DOLLAR
Composition: 77% copper, 12% zinc, 7%
manganese, 4% nickel
Years: 2000-Current
Weight: 8.1 Grams
Diameter: 26.5mm

1971-D Peg Leg

Look at: The R in LIBERTY on the obverse.
Look for: The bottom left portion of the R is not present.

VALUE:

Extra Fine	About Uncirculated	Uncirculated
5.00	9.00	15.00

A newly discovered copy of this variety displays a minor doubled reverse — you may become lucky and discover two varieties on one coin! The coin with both features may be worth $30-$50.

> **Listing Numbers**
> When referring to the "Peg-Leg" the coin should be described as the date and "peg-leg." *Example: 1971-D Business Strike Peg-Leg.*

COIN COURTESY OF: Brian Allen

PHOTO COURTESY OF: Brian Allen

1971-S Peg Leg+Doubled Die Obverse

Look at: The R in LIBERTY on the obverse.
Look for: The bottom left portion of the R is not present.

VALUE:

Extra Fine	About Uncirculated	Uncirculated
10.00	20.00	45.00

This "Peg-Leg" business strike also features a doubled obverse, which may be difficult to detect to the untrained eye. If you do find the "peg-leg" in circulation, chances are the doubled die is present as well. However, there are two known Peg-legs in circulation for the 1971-S Eisenhower Dollars.

> **Listing Numbers**
> CONECA: DDO-009
> Potter:VCR#1/DDO#1
> Wexler: WDDO-007

The lower serif on this coin is completely missing.

COIN COURTESY OF: James Sego

PHOTO COURTESY OF: Kevin Flynn

Look at: The R in LIBERTY on the obverse.
Look for: The bottom left portion of the R is not present.

VALUE:

Extra Fine	About Uncirculated	Uncirculated
4.00	8.00	15.00

Normal appearing R of LIBERTY on the EISENHOWER DOLLAR.

COINS COURTESY OF: Brian Allen   *PHOTOS COURTESY OF:* Brian Allen

Look at: The earth on the top left side of the reverse.

Look for: Look for a long "flattened" string of Islands below Florida. Normal coins will show three very distinct Islands; the proof style reverse will have one long "group."

Listing Numbers
Common descriptions:
Proof Reverse
Type II Reverse
Type B Reverse

VALUE:

Extra Fine	About Uncirculated	Uncirculated
80.00	125.00	250.00+

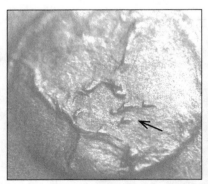

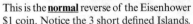

This is the **normal** reverse of the Eisenhower $1 coin. Notice the 3 short defined Islands.

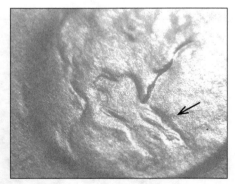

This is the rare Proof reverse that was accidentally struck on circulation coins from the 1972-P Eisenhower dollars. This is easy to detect and very valuable.

If you were fortunate enough to find this rare variety in a very high grade, the value could be over $1000. It is rare but can be found by looking at the islands below Florida. Use the comparative photos to begin recognition of what looks normal and the proof reverse will stand out even better when you see it!

COIN COURTESY OF: Ken Jones   *PHOTO COURTESY OF: Brian Allen*

Look at: You will need a scale to determine this variety.
Look for: A coin that weighs 24.59 grams. The correct weight should be 22.68 grams.

VALUE:

Extra Fine	About Uncirculated	Uncirculated	Heritage 1999, Chicago ANA Sale.
1200.00	3500.00	5500.00	

If you do not have a scale at home, try the post office or a local jeweler. Larger post offices have a digital scale located in the lobby for weighing packages at no cost. The only absolute method of determining if this coin is a silver-clad is by conducting a specific gravity test, these type tests can often be conducted in high school or college science rooms, but the specific gravity test is also offered by several attributers of major error dealers and clubs. You will not be able to sell this variety without proof that the specific gravity and weight are that of the silver-clad.

A suspect coin *may* have a shiny reflective finish, much like silver coinage. The first step to helping you with identifying this coin is to use the "tissue-overlay" method shown in Chapter 9. You will not be able to determine the silver content on the Kennedy Half-Dollars or the Eisenhower Dollars by looking for the sandwich colors on the rim of the coin for these errors are composed of 40% silver and not 90% like the Roosevelt Dime and Washington Quarter errors.

The second step to identify the variety is to weigh the coin. The weight of the silver-clad error will be 24.59 grams and the clad coinage will weigh 22.68 grams. The difference is very minor and could be misleading. The only true method of determination is by performing a specific gravity test to determine the metal composition. This test, although not extremely complicated, is time consuming.

PHOTO COURTESY OF: Heritage Coin Gallery

Look at: You will need a scale, although the R of LIBERTY on the obverse and the R of AMERICA on the reverse can assist you with narrowing your search.

Look for: A coin that weighs 24.59 grams. The correct weight should be 22.68 grams. There are no serifs on the bottom leg of the R in LIBERTY.

VALUE:

Extra Fine	About Uncirculated	Uncirculated
750.00	1000.00	2000.00

Notice the bottom tip of the R DOES NOT touch the I in AMERICA. This is the style R that is featured on the valuable error.

Notice the bottom tip of the R DOES touch the I in AMERICA. This style R is NOT on the valuable error.

You will encounter two types of variations on the front and back of the 1976D. The variety shown here is currently known on the type we have shown here. The photos shown above do not mean that you have found a silver-clad variety, but assist you in determining the need to conduct further test.

Use the same detection procedures for this silver-clad error as you use for the previously listed 1974D and the 1977D (next page) and the "tissue overlay" procedure shown on the page 225.

PHOTO COURTESY OF: Brian Allen
Due to the rarity of this variety, the above photo is of a normal coin.

Look at: You will need a scale to determine this variety.
Look for: An Ike dollar that appears to be made of silver.

VALUE:

Extra Fine	About Uncirculated	Uncirculated
1000.00	2000.00	3500.00

If you do not have a scale at home, try the post office or a local jeweler. Larger post offices have a digital scale located in the lobby for weighing packages, at no cost. The only absolute method of determining if this coin is a silver-clad is by conducting a specific gravity test, these type test can often be conducted in high school or college science rooms, but the specific gravity test is also offered by several attributers of major error dealers and clubs. You will not be able to sell this variety without proof that the specific gravity and weight are that of the silver-clad.

A suspect coin *may* have a shiny reflective finish, much like silver coinage. The first step to helping you with identifying this coin is to use the "tissue-overlay" method shown in Chapter 9. You will not be able to determine the silver content on the Kennedy Half-Dollars or the Eisenhower Dollars by looking for the sandwich colors on the rim of the coin for these errors are composed of 40% silver and not 90% like the Roosevelt Dime and Washington Quarter errors.

The second step to identify the variety is to weigh the coin. The weight of the silver-clad error will be 24.59 grams and the clad coinage will weigh 22.68 grams. The difference is very minor and could be misleading. The only true method of determination is by performing a specific gravity test to determine the metal composition. This test, although not extremely complicated, is time consuming.

PHOTO COURTESY OF: Brian Allen
Due to the rarity of this variety, the above photo is of a normal coin.

Look at: The distance between the bottom of the numbers of the date and the rim.

Look for: A wide rim with the date close to the border. The 1 will almost be touching the rim. This is the same date and rim used in 1980, 1981 and 1999.

VALUE:

Extra Fine	About Uncirculated	Uncirculated
8.00	15.00	25.00

The key to locating this variety is the distance of the rim from the bottom letters of the date. The more valuable variety will not have a wide gap between the numbers and the rim. Additionally notice the very wide or "deep" rim.

Narrow Rim-"FAR-DATE"

This is the common and normal-appearing rim. Notice the gap between the bottom of the numbers in 1979 and the rim. To get a better idea of how to identify this variety, look at 1980 or 1981 Susan B Anthony dollars; they both feature the narrow gap between the rim and the date.

> **Listing Numbers**
> Breen#5834   Cherrypickers':FS-016   Potter:VCR#2/ODV#1

PHOTO COURTESY OF: JT Stanton

Look at: The color of the coin.

Look for: A Susan B Anthony dollar that has accidentally struck on a blank coin intended for use on the 2000 Sacagawea Golden Dollar.

VALUE:

Extra Fine	About Uncirculated	Uncirculated
3500.00	5,000.00	15,000.00

The above photo is a representation of the Susan B. Anthony struck on a Sacagawea Planchet. A photo of an authentic specimen was offered for use in this publication; however, due to technical difficulties, we were unable to use the photographs. The original photos were offered by Mike Byers.

This variety should be easy to detect! However, be extremely careful when purchasing as this type of error could be easily faked by plating a normal Susan B. Anthony with gold.

Look at: The color of the coin.
Look for: A 2000 Sacagawea Golden Dollar that has accidentally struck on a blank coin intended for use on the Susan B Anthony Dollar.

VALUE:

Extra Fine	About Uncirculated	Uncirculated
3,500.00	5,000.00	15,000.00

The above photo is a representation of the Susan B. Anthony struck on a Sacagawea Planchet. A photo of an authentic specimen was offered for use in this publication; however, due to technical difficulties, we were unable to use the photographs. The original photos were offered by Mike Byers.

Look at: The new 2000-P Golden Dollar Reverses.

Look for: A reverse that is rotated from the normal position.

VALUE:

Extra Fine	About Uncirculated	Uncirculated
-	200.00	500.00

There are several different rotations known for the 2000-P, including 90, 135 and 180 degrees. The prices shown above are listed for 180 degree rotations. Less degree rotations will command lesser values.

ABOUT EISENHOWER AND SUSAN B. ANTHONY
DOLLAR VALUABLES

The dollar series has never had a strong backing of the general public and has not been a highly collected denomination among collectors. The dollar varieties have begun to grow slowly in popularity, particularly the transitional pieces of off metals. The error coins such as off-centers, major die breaks, and clips have always been in high demand and will only continue to gain strength.

Some people will argue that you do not find dollar denominations in your pocket change. They are correct. However if you are looking for a denomination, go to your local bank and buy $25-$100 worth of Ike dollars and examine them closely for a few of the doubled obverses or off metals that we have listed in this text. If you find nothing of interest take them back to the bank and your efforts will have cost you nothing. Although one good find will lend you a few extra dollars.

Look closely at the IN GOD WE TRUST on Eisenhower Dollars, there are dozens of doubled dies that are evident on the obverse and nearly as many on the reverse.

WHAT IS THIS?

The *Sacagawea One Dollar Coin* was ordered under the United States Dollar Coin Act of 1997. As part of this act, the US Congress required that the new dollar coin meet the following requirements: be golden in **color**, have a distinctive edge, and be the same 26.5mm diameter as the current Susan B. Anthony Dollar. The Secretary of the Treasury also required that the Sacagawea Dollar's obverse and reverse designs consist of: an obverse that showed one or more women (cannot be of a living person) and the reverse must depict an eagle.

Physical Characteristics

The Golden Dollar weighs 8.1 grams, 2 mm thick, and 26.5 mm in diameter.

The coin is composed of three layers — pure copper between (and bonded) to two outer layers of manganese brass. The Sacagawea Dollar's complete metal composition is: 88.5% copper, 6.0% zinc, 3.5% manganese and 2% nickel. There is NO amount of Gold in the new dollar, only golden in color.

Strike It Rich With Pocket Change

Finding Errors
An Interesting Alternative

Errors and varieties are classified into three main divisions: Planchet, Die, and Striking errors and varieties. This classification system is commonly referred to as the "PDS System" (which represents the first initial of each of the three main classifications).

While the main focus of this book is the die varieties and errors that can easily slip past the watchful inspector's eye or circumvent mechanical screening devices, there are certain error types that fall into the "planchet error" and "striking error" divisions that occasionally get into circulation that are of interest to collectors. These types are generally of normal or near-normal dimensions, allowing them to pass through the mechanical screening systems that eliminate the majority of errors that are undersize, out-of-round, or otherwise misshapen. Let's take a closer look.

Planchet Errors and Varieties

Planchet errors and varieties obviously involve a mishap or deliberate change affecting the planchet the coin is struck on. Although a "blank" is not the same thing as a "planchet" — for our purposes it is treated as a planchet within the context of the classification system for errors. (A blank is the raw disc of metal punched from out of coinage strip; a blank becomes a planchet once it has been run through the upset mill to raise the rim, making it ready for striking.)

Our first coin is an example of the so-called "Curved Clip" which is the most common of the "Incomplete Planchet" errors. It's represented by the 1988-D Kennedy half dollar which actually displays a total of three curved clips. The term "clip" is a misnomer that errorists tend to accept in describing a general class of planchet error that originates with a blank that was produced with an incomplete area of metal at its edge. The curved clip occurs when a blank is punched from out of an area of strip that overlaps a hole (or holes) from where a blank was previously punched out.

Envision using a cookie cutter used to "punch" out a cookie from an area of rolled out dough that overlaps into an area from where you have already cut out a cookie, and it's easy to understand how the "curved clip" errors occur.

The flat area of the rim opposite the "Curved Clip" on the 1994-D Kennedy half is known in the hobby as the "Blaksley Effect." It is the result of an absence of pressure in the area opposite the clip during the rimming or upsetting process. If a portion of a blank is of an insufficient diameter to make complete contact with the grooves of the upset mill, no pressure will be present when the clip is in the pinch-point position and an upset will not occur in the affected areas. When an upset fails to occur in the area opposite the clip, it will often remain flat in that area after the strike. This is considered one of several authentication points on a genuine "Incomplete Planchet" error — though its absence does not necessarily deem it a fake. Since this type of error is easily simulated through alteration of a normal coin, professional authentication is recommended.

The "Straight Clip" occurs when the edge of the coinage strip is punched from the side or the end of the strip. Our 1981-P Jefferson nickel is a perfect example of this error type. It also features a "Curved Clip" opposite the "Straight Clip."

Strike It Rich With Pocket Change

The 1980 Lincoln cent shown is known as an "Elliptical Clip" and is a relatively rare form of clip. It occurs when a blank is produced while overlapping an area of strip that was previously punched but with the previous blank still intact in the hole due to insufficient shearing. This mishap will produce a blank with a partially punched curved shear running thru its interior that will become two errors if it breaks apart; the "elliptical" and a regular "curved clip."

Our Roosevelt Dime from 196? is a "Ragged Clip." The ragged clip is a form of "Lamination." Laminations are usually due to contaminants or gasses trapped within the metal causing it to split, peel, crack, or even form holes. In this case the lamination was at the edge resulting in the "ragged edge" effect. While this one is on a foreign coin, the type is often found on US coins.

When lamination is severe enough to pass entirely through the coinage strip and is then punched out orientated somewhere entirely within the confines of the coin's rim, it is affectionately known by collectors as a "blow hole"—a term borrowed from the welding trade. Our 1962 Lincoln cent shows a beautiful example of this rare error type. I found this one while searching through a Mint bag several years ago.

Surface laminations are referred to as "Lamination Peels," "Lamination Cracks," or simply as laminations (usually in conjunction with a modifier indicating their depth). Our 1969-D Kennedy half exhibits a fairly deep lamination in the proximity of the IB of LIBERTY. Laminations of this type are rare on clad coins.

Our next coin is another form of lamination on an undated Lincoln Memorial cent that was struck on a "Split Planchet." In this case the entire planchet split horizontally and separated from the other half before it was struck. This particular coin also qualifies as a "Multiple Error" with the second error falling into the "Striking Category" of the PDS System. At about 9 o'clock we can see this coin was accompanied into the dies by yet another planchet that overlapped by about 15%+ and was struck off-center. The weakness of strike on this error is diagnostic of the type and is due to a lack of metal to strike up.

Due to improper bonding, it is possible for an entire clad layer to split completely away from the copper core of our modern clad coinage. Our 1998-P Roosevelt dime shown here features a 100% missing clad layer resulting in a "copper reverse." In this case we can see that the missing clad layer fell away before the coin was struck since both sides show a complete design. If the clad layer had broken away after the strike, the reverse would be missing most of the design (save for some faint image). Weakness of strike is diagnostic to the error type when the clad layer falls away before the strike (due to insufficient metal to strike up), but this one is a better than average in strike.

Even rarer than the missing clad layer error is finding a struck clad layer itself. The outer layer of copper-nickel occasionally breaks away from the copper core of a clad planchet and is struck independent of the core. At other times a clad layer is struck with all layers intact and breaks away later. The weakness of strike is typical of the error type when the clad layer is struck alone; the date is often undeterminable on such strikes. The cause of the error is improper bonding which may be due to a variety of factors including trapped coolant, oxidation between layers, and/or other contaminants.

Striking Errors

The Striking Error class includes the majority of obvious eye-appealing errors such as: off-metals, off-centers, double-denominations, brockages, etc. As the name implies, this class occurs during the mechanical process of striking the coin. Many of the errors in this class are misshapen and will not pass through counting machines or fit into rolls and are thus not normally encountered by the average collector looking through pocket change. As such, we will concentrate on types that are of the sort that do turn up in pocket change and defer the reader interested in the weirder mistrikes to the chapter in "States Quarters" errors.

Our first striking error is the "Indent Strike." It occurs when two planchets overlap each other and are struck together in that orientation. Usually the lower planchet is fully centered in the collar and is referred to as the indent strike while the upper coin is an off center with uniface reverse. The 1970-D Washington shows us a rare form of indent. It's indented by a clad shell that broke away from a planchet and managed to hitchhike its way part way into the dies with this coin. The 1997 Washington quarter to follow is even rarer and is indented by a complete Roosevelt dime planchet.

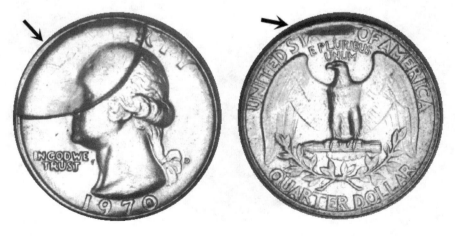

Strike It Rich With Pocket Change

The ever-popular "off-metal" and "wrong-planchet" strikes occur when the planchets of the wrong denomination, or even those intended for a different country's coinage, are fed into a press and struck in error. Our 1979 Jefferson nickel was struck on a cent planchet while our 1999-D cent was struck in a silver-colored foreign planchet.

One of the most dramatic and highly collectable of the striking errors is the "double denomination." As the name implies, the error involves the striking of a planchet by the dies of two different denominations. Our 1991 cent struck on a dime (known as an 11c piece), was first struck normally by ten-cent dies and was then struck a second time by one-cent dies. This one is known as a "flip-over double strike" because the ten-cent design was struck by the one-cent dies, reverse to obverse.

Photo courtesy of Alan Herbert.

This 1991 Lincoln Cent was struck on a 10c piece with Lincoln's front on the back of the dime. This is called a "Flip-over" double strike.

This 1999 Lincoln Cent was struck on a 10c piece with Lincoln's front on the front of the dime.

Our 1964-D Lincoln cent displays a beautiful example of the so-called "Die Trial," or "Die Adjustment Strike" or what I prefer to call a "Weak Strike." Undoubtedly some weak strikes occur after dies have been set and the pressure is gradually adjusted upward until sufficient to fill the details of the die. Early strikes from this process are very weak and gradually get correspondingly stronger as the pressure is increased. Other factors, such as the shutting down of a press or a loss of hydraulics (amongst others) have been identified as possible causes of weak strikes. Coins that are just a bit weakly struck command no premium while

very weak strikes can command significant premiums. The cent shown here is worth about $60 while the 197? Kennedy half is worth about $200.00

As is typical in most manufacturing environments, stray pieces of broken tooling, cleaning cloths, threads, lint, bristles from wire brushes, etc. can and will fall within the dies and get struck into coins. Our first example of the "Strike Thru" error is an undated Lincoln cent struck through cloth. This coin is worth about $75.00 to $100.00. Our second example is a 1981-D cent struck through a bristle from a wire brush or what is known as a "file card" inside the Mint. While the stray objects that get struck into coins often fall out later, this coin still has the wire retained and makes it worth all the more. This one is worth about $100.00.

Another form of "Strike Thru" error is the "Brockage." The brockage error occurs when a coin sticks or "caps" the upper die and begins to act as a die itself. It will then strike incoming planchets until it drops off or wears itself so thin that it literally deteriorates to nothing. Each strike from a cap causes it to spread and wrap itself up higher on the shank of the die. The more strikes it receives, the deeper the cap and the further design detail spreads outward. Each coin struck with the cap will show a progressive spread of design image until it is no longer identifiable and it thins out to a point the lower die's image begins to show through. Early stage specimens are very fairly scarce and very desirable to collectors. Later stages are also highly collectable. Shown are examples of Brockages in about the mid-stage.

There are many more errors and variety types that we are unable to elaborate upon within the scope of this chapter. However, if we have whet your appetite for errors and you'd like to learn more about them and the clubs and books dedicated to their study, please check the appropriate chapters to aid you in this goal.

A Different Error Possibility...........

The photos shown below are of a variety known as a "CUD" or "Die Break." They may be found on any denomination and come in various sizes and shapes. Value will depend accordingly.

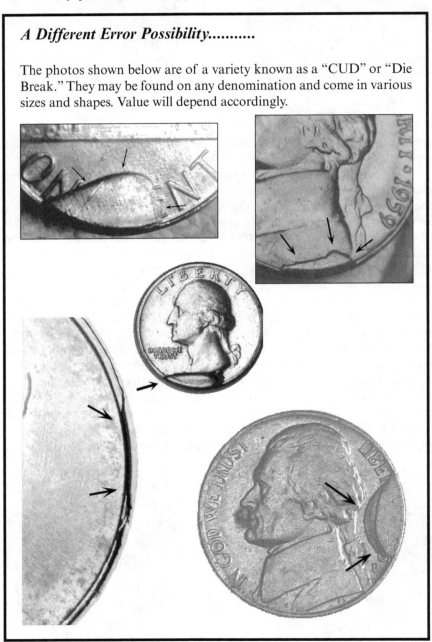

BRASS PLATED LINCOLN CENTS

This error was described (in reference to 1985-D strikes of the same type) in a June 27, 1985 letter from Jerry Yellin, Chief, Assay Division - U.S. Mint where he indicated that the difference in color is due to the amount of zinc in the copper plating. In a properly plated cent there would be no zinc in the outer layer. He explained that it is not uncommon for several zinc blanks to be retained in the plating tanks. After a period of time the blanks begin dissolving and contaminate the plating solution (electrolyte). Thus a brass plating rather than a copper plating is formed on subsequent blanks to be plated.

Of course the number of retained blanks and their stage of decomposition will affect the amount of zinc contamination and thus the depth of the yellowish-brass color of each strike examined. As the decomposition progresses, the more yellow the coins struck from affected planchets. Previous years of notable brass plated cents (1983, 1983-D, 1985, 1985-D and 1997-D) have had a wide range of color contrast between the standard copper plated examples and the brass plated specimens, ranging from barely noticeable to a very obvious yellow coloration with the greatest range of contrast found on the 1983 and 1985-D issues (some of the 1985-D issues were nearly as yellow as gold).

Authentication is recommended for this variety as the brassy effects can be simulated.

Finding States Quarter Errors!
A Unique Opportunity

A unique area of opportunity available to collectors of error coins is in the unsearched bags of "Statehood Commemorative Quarters" that the United States Mint has been selling direct to collectors since the launch of that program in 1999. Unsearched bags can also be obtained through private dealers. While the vast majority of odd-size or otherwise mis-shapen errors get caught by the Mint's inspection and sorting processes, a few do escape the system into bulk bags of coin. Normally, most of those "escapees" get caught by privately operated coin wrapping operations during the process of rolling the coins into the familiar tubes we see in cash drawers. Those persons, in turn, supply error dealers with most of the new errors that we see offered each year.

The Mint's decision to sell these quarters in bulk, direct to the collector, means that the valuable error coins that banks and other coin wrapping operations virtually monopolized upon for decades, are now available to you! While Mint-sewn bags of coin have always been available, collectors often had to know the right person in a bank or have a large enough account to be granted the favor of obtaining a few of these bags. The alternative was to purchase them from dealers at hefty premiums, which in the current market must be viewed as "reasonable" since these bags have been steadily increasing in value. Today, unsearched bags of States quarters can be obtained directly from the Mint for a modest fee plus shipping charges. Each bag represents an opportunity of possibly finding a valuable error coin (or more) that could net you hundreds or even thousands of dollars!

These bags represent a golden opportunity to the collector because the bulk sales program comes at a time when more errors than ever are being produced (due to high coinage output demands on the Mint), and at a time when State quarter errors are, unquestionably, the most active area in the error coin market. While it might at first seem that increased supplies of errors would be counterproductive to the market, the fact is they represent a significant number of diverse error types — some very rare — that have been well distributed amongst the commemorative designs introduced thus far (five State quarter designs are being issued each year for ten years). Furthermore, each design represents a one-year-of-type or perhaps what, one observer states, might be better described as "two-months-of-issue-type," since most of the designs are struck within 30 to 45 production days or "within two-months." This virtually guarantees that almost as quickly as the supply of one state design enters the market, it will end abruptly and the supply of the next Statehood issue will begin. Even more importantly, many error collectors collect by type, i.e., one of each of their favorite error types on each denomination and design. Thus what at first seems like a large number will be minuscule when one compares the total mintage on any one of the States Commemorative quarter designs to that of all dates for the regular issue clad-date Washington quarters.

In this chapter, we show some of the States quarter error coins that have been found thus far along with a brief description of how each occurred and an approximate estimate of what it is worth. It needs to be emphasized that values of error coins can range greatly depending on the dealer handling them and the individual characteristics of the coins. One dealer may place a greater value on a certain error type than another based solely on his/her preferences or a knowledge that he/she has the clientele to support the price attached. Furthermore, while there may be many similar errors within a given type, most errors are one-of-a-kind and prices will be based on each coin's individual characteristics and eye appeal. The prices quoted here represent estimates given to us by two of the nation's largest error coin dealers for the specific coins shown.

200   *Strike It Rich With Pocket Change*

Our first coin is a 1999-P New Jersey quarter that is Double Struck with both strikes Off-Center. The first strike is off-center by about 15% while the second strike overlaps into the first strike and blank area. The second strike is about 80% off-center and occurred while the coin was resting on top of another blank. This caused the reverse to display a stretched out, distorted image of the original strike in that area or what is referred to in the hobby as "Uniface Reverse." It is valued at approximately $650 to $700.

The 1999-P Pennsylvania quarter displays a nice Straight Clip of about 15% at 11:30. Straight clips are a form of "Incomplete Planchet" error and occur when the blank is punched out from either side of the end of the coinage strip. (A "planchet" is a blank that has been processed to have its rim raised slightly and is ready for striking into a coin.) This error is less spectacular than many of the others shown here, but it appears to be quite rare on this series and is a highly sought after type. It is valued at approximately $100.

COIN COURTESY OF: Fred Weinberg

This spectacular 1999-P Georgia commemorative piece is a dramatic quadruple strike! The first strike was normal while a succession of three closely overlapping, off-center strikes battered the coin before it was finally ejected from the coining chamber. The tripling of the trio of off-center strikes is best viewed on the tops of UNITED. It is worth approximately $850 to $950.

COIN COURTESY OF: Fred Weinberg

The 1999-? New Jersey piece shown here was struck off-center by about 20% while another coin was resting partially on top creating a huge indented area with an incuse mirror design of the reverse within. This multiple error coin is known as an Off-Center with Partial Brockage. The extra thickness of metal from both the coin and the planchet being struck together caused the planchet to split adding just a bit more eye appeal to this "mess." This one is worth from about $375 to $550.

COIN COURTESY OF: Ken Potter

The 1999-P Pennsylvania quarter shows the image of both the obverse and reverse on both sides. The ghostly image below the strong image is the result of this coin having been struck once and then flipping over and reentering the coining press for a second on-center strike. This one is referred to as Double Struck Flipover In Collar and is valued at about $700.

COIN COURTESY OF: Fred Weinberg

Here is a 1999-P Connecticut quarter that was partially indented by another struck coin (apparently another error coin) that fell part way into the dies during the strike. This is known as a Partial Brockage and worth from about $190 to $250.

Next we show a 1999-? New Jersey quarter that was Double Struck with Both Strikes Off-Center. The larger of the two strikes exhibits an area with a flat edge known as a "Chain Edge," a reference alluding to the "linking" of this coin to another. This occurs when two non-overlapping planchets enter partially into the coining chamber in an off center position and are struck simultaneously. Under the pressure of the strike, the metal from both planchets begins to flow in all directions including toward each other. When the metal flowing from both planchets meets, resistance is created and the flow of metal is redirected resulting in the chain edge effect seen on a small percentage of off centers and double strikes. This one is worth from about $550 to $650 "as is" but would be worth about $850 if it was scratch-free.

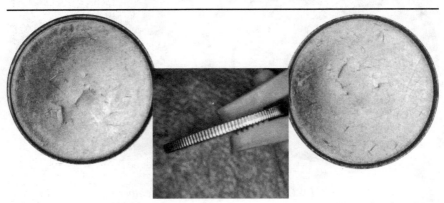

Here we show yet another 1999-? New Jersey quarter. This one was struck with Filled Dies. In this case the dies were clogged with grease or other contaminants thus preventing the dies from imparting complete designs to the blank. This error type is easily confused with a Weak Strike but an examination of the edge of the coin shows that it has fully struck reeding that could have occurred only if the coin was struck with normal pressure. This one is valued from $40 to $300.

Strike It Rich With Pocket Change

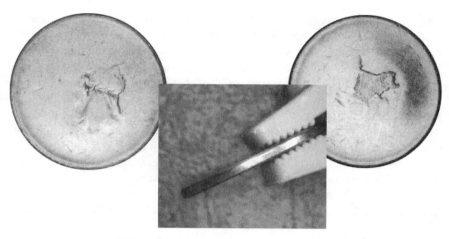

COIN COURTESY OF: Fred Weinberg

To illustrate this point further, our next coin is a Weak Strike on a (2000)-? Massachusetts quarter. Notice that not only is the area of design detail on the obverse (Washington side) and reverse extremely weak but the reeding on the edge is nonexistent. This one is worth about $400 to $450.

COIN COURTESY OF: Ken Potter

COIN COURTESY OF: Chuck Avery

An odd-ball that has been appearing in increasing frequency is the "Clad Layer Missing Before Strike" error. It is represented by the 1999-P Georgia and 1999-D Delaware quarters with a "copper obverse" and "copper reverse," respectively. This error occurs when a blank sheds one of its outer copper-nickel "clad" layers before it is struck. When struck, the side missing the outer layer will be copper while the flip side will be of the normal copper-nickel (silvery) appearance. A clad layer may split off if it is improperly bonded due to contaminants or oxides being trapped between the layers during the bonding process. This error type is worth about $250 to $300 in uncirculated condition. Many of these have been reported on all the State designs as being found in circulation or fresh out of new rolls. They are worth less if circulated. (Note: The yellowish cast seen on the obverse of the Georgia quarter and the reverse of the Delaware quarter are due to the scanning process. They are actually of the normal clad "silvery" appearance.)

COIN COURTESY OF: Fred Weinberg

This 1999-P Connecticut quarter displays two large curved clips. The term "clip" is a misnomer that errorists tend to accept in describing a general class of planchet error that originates with a blank that was produced with an incomplete area of metal at its edge. The curved clip occurs when a blank is punched from out of an area of strip that overlaps a hole (or holes) from where a blank was previously punched out.

Envision using a cookie cutter to "punch" out a cookie from an area of rolled out dough that overlaps into an area from where cookies were previously cut out. In this case the blank was punched out from are area overlapping two holes. It is valued at about $125.

Our next coin is a 2000-D Massachusetts quarter that was struck Off-Center on a blank with Double Curved Clips. In this case, the clips probably caused the blank to misfeed, causing this spectacular multiple error type. It is valued at approximately $350 but would be worth over $500 if scratch free.

This 1999-D New Jersey quarter exhibits a "Corner Clip" or what some refer to as an "Assay Clip." This is the result of a piece of metal being snipped from the coinage strip (in the proximity of where the blank was later punched) for testing. The test may be for assay or to check metal hardness or ductility. This is an extremely rare error type with this one boasting a value ranging from about $400 to $650. This error type is so rare it is difficult to price.

COIN COURTESY OF: Fred Weinberg

This States quarter is Double Struck with a Brockaged reverse. The brockage is from the obverse of another coin being impressed into this coin during the strike. This prevents us from determining which of the State's quarter designs it represents. The date and Mint mark are also unknown due to the orientation of the strikes. Still, the error is so dramatic that it would fetch anywhere from about $550 to $850 in the open market.

COIN COURTESY OF: Fred Weinberg

This 2000-D Massachusetts quarter was struck Off-center by about 10% to 12%. An off-center strike occurs when a planchet fails to enter the striking chamber in a centered position. While it is not as major as some of the other striking errors featured here, it is still a very desirable coin with an affordable value of about $125 to $200.

COIN COURTESY OF: Fred Weinberg

In sharp contrast to our 10% off-center featured previously, this States quarter of unknown date and type, was struck about 95% Off-Center. Even though dated pieces struck in the 40% to 60% range are the most desirable to collectors, this one would still command a respectable $100 to $150 if sold to a collector. It would be worth $200 plus if the State could be determined.

COIN COURTESY OF:
Frank LaBosco

COIN COURTESY OF: Jack Martin

So far everything we've looked at has involved an error in the striking of the coin or preparation of the blank. However, errors and varieties can occur to the dies. While recent innovations within the Mint have largely eliminated the possibility of the popular Doubled Dies and Repunched Mint Mark varieties from occurring, minor die variations (often erroneously referred to as "minor errors") such as die chips and/or die breaks, die cracks, missing designs due to die-wear and/or abrasion, doubling due to die-deterioration, etc., still occur and are considered collectable by some segments of the hobby. Shown here is a 1999-P Pennsylvania quarter with a large die break between the U and E of VIRTUE. It was found by Frank LaBosco in March of 1999. Also shown is a 1999-P Delaware quarter with die breaks between the A and R of CAESAR and within the lower N of RODNEY. It was found by Jack Martin in March of 1999. Items like these shown have been selling for about $2 while die cracks, missing designs, die deterioration doubling, etc., normally sell for considerably less (depending on the State involved).

THE ROTATED REVERSE

Last but not least are the "Rotated Die Errors." This error type involves the instillation of one of the dies into a press in the wrong rotational alignment, or for one of the dies to break loose from its fixed position allowing it to rotate within the die holder. Normally, the dies for United States coins will be set into the press with their designs opposite each other, shifted toward opposite poles. This will result in a struck coin that will show the obverse right side up while the reverse is up-side-down. This is normal and referred to as "coin alignment." However, on rare occasions, one of the dies is set so that it strikes coins in an orientation other than "coin alignment." This can result in a coin that if held with its obverse upright, will display the reverse at any alignment other than the proper 180° "coin alignment." The most desirable error of this type is one that shows a 180° misalignment, which of course results in a coin with no rotational differentiation between the obverse and reverse (or what is referred to as "medal alignment" since most commemorative medals, military medals, and tokens are struck in this manner).

To date, at least five different States quarter designs have been found with significant "Rotated Die" errors. Any rotational misalignment of over 15% is considered significant.

ESTIMATED VALUE:	DEGREE OF REVERSE ROTATION		
	25-50	**50-90**	**90-180**
Lincoln Cents	5.00	20.00	60.00
Jefferson Nickels	8.00	25.00	80.00
Roosevelt Dimes	?	?	?
Washington Quarters	35.00	75.00	200.00
Kennedy Half-Dollars	60.00	150.00	350.00
Ike/SBA Dollars	?	?	?
Sacagawea Dollars	125.00	250.00	500.00

CIRCULATION DATES WITH KNOWN 90-180 DEGREE ROTATIONS

Lincoln Cents	Jefferson Nickels	Washington Quarters	Half-Dollars
1966	1966	1965	1973-D
1972-D	1969-S	1966	1979-D
1973-D		1972-D	1984-D
1993-D		1985	1988-P
1994		1989-P	
		1999-P & D	

There are many more error and variety types that we are unable to elaborate upon within the scope of this article. However, if this article has whet your appetite for errors and you'd like to learn more about them and the clubs and books dedicated to their study, you may contact me at my email address listed below or with a long self-addressed envelope and 99¢ postage; I'll send you all that you need to get started. Request the "Error Coin Starter Kit."

*****Although we only show photos for three denominations, the rules for Rotated Reverse applies to all U.S. coin denominations.*

Another Error possibility.....

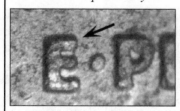

The photo on the right shows a clear E of E PLURIBUS UNUM that was struck into the steps of the Memorial building.

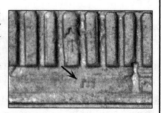

This Lincoln Cent error is known as a "Dropped Letter," a form of lamination created when a portion of the coin (with a letter) peeled away from the planchet and fell onto the die. The "dropped" featured will always be incused (not raised). This type of error is uncommon and difficult to locate; therefore, values are hard to estimate.

Coin Courtesy: Mike DeCarter

Buying and Selling Error-Variety Coins

If you've read this far, it can be assumed that you have garnered enough interest in the subject to have already started looking through your pocket change. In time, you'll have accumulated a pile of coins, some of which you may have properly attributed and are ready to "cash in." Or perhaps you've been bitten by the "bug" and want to collect these "oddities" and are interested in buying some of the varieties you cannot find. Either way, you'll eventually need to know where to buy and sell error-variety coins. (For the sake of simplicity, we will restrict this chapter to "selling" your finds, but note that the same information is of equal value to those who wish to buy, sell, or trade.)

You'll quickly learn that error-variety coin collecting is an obscure specialty to most dealers in the trade; they will either offer you a pittance or not be interested in buying them at all. If you are lucky, they will suggest a dealer or club that specializes in this area.

Yet there are thousands of collectors out there interested in acquiring your coins and there is a network of dealers in place to serve their needs. The trick to selling your coins is to learn who these dealers and collectors are, and how to come into contact with them.

First, you need to determine how you want to sell your coins. There are essentially three avenues you can take: Selling to dealers, selling direct to collectors, and sales through auctions. All of these routes have certain advantages and disadvantages.

Selling to dealers has the advantage in that you are finished with the job of marketing the coins at the moment you cash the dealer's check. The dealer will now have to find the individual customers for these items and handle all the details associated with each transaction. This will include the obvious (such as properly packaging the coins, invoicing, and shipping) to the not-so-obvious (researching the prices, grading the coins, the writing of ads, creating and mailing catalogs, issuing press releases, getting the coins certified by grading services, etc.). Selling to dealers also offers the distinct advantage of having a qualified examiner to double check your coins to make sure they are what you think they are.

Make no mistake, your most critical concern must be to deal in properly attributed coins. There are many forms of doubling that mimic the collectable forms — these look-a-likes are virtually worthless. A coin soaked in acid for a length of time will be undersize and may appear to be a coin struck on the wrong blank. Hundreds of these turn up each year from persons convinced they found a rare and valuable error coin. Coins with two heads or two tails are "Magician's coins," created by lathing two coins into one. They are worth little more than the two or three dollars they fetched in the novelty shop from where they originate, and not an error coin of interest to the hobbyist. If you get caught selling these as valuable errors, your reputation will suffer and you will soon find that word-of-mouth has eliminated you from the list of reputable dealers.

It is strongly suggested that you become thoroughly familiar with the various types of collectable varieties and errors before you start dealing in them. Thus it is sometimes best to start your "career" in this area by selling through dealers where you can obtain an education before venturing out to sell direct to collectors or through auctions.

To find dealers who specialize in this area, start by looking at the ads in this book. Only reputable dealers, qualified to deal in this area were invited to advertise here. Second, try looking through the advertisements, including the classified section of any of the major numismatic periodicals (*Coin World* and *Numismatic News*, *COINage*, etc.), and through specialty magazines published by error-variety coin clubs or by commercial concerns. The dealer ads in the classified section will usually be larger and set in a "display format," i.e., with fancier type, various font sizes, centering, etc. It is important to distinguish dealers from private collectors if you are interested in selling in bulk, as collectors normally only buy what they need while dealers will usually buy everything that is considered saleable within fairly broad categories.

When contacting dealers it is best to do so by phone as you can quickly ascertain their level of interest in the type of material you offer. Some dealers only handle major striking and planchet errors, such as Off Center strikes and Clips, while others deal exclusively in die variations such as those found in the bulk of this book. Still others handle a little bit of everything.

If you decide to write, make sure you send a self-addressed stamped envelope if you expect a reply. It is also important for you to enclose a detailed letter explaining what you have along with some reference to this book or other books that will suggest that you have something worthwhile.

The fact is, error-variety dealers receive dozens of inquiries every week from folks that have little more than common non-collectable forms of doubling or alterations that they are attempting to sell or learn more about. Regrettably, most of these inquiries end up in the dealers trash can with no answer because most folks do not extend the courtesy of including a self-addressed stamped envelope, and they provide too little information for the dealer to determine whether or not the prospect has anything worth buying. Dealers know from experience that most inquiries in regard to selling error coins result in no purchases or a spinning of their wheels over "junk" that nobody wants. If you extend the courtesy of a self-addressed envelope and demonstrate some knowledge in the subject, you will probably receive a favorable reply. Contact may also be made via email with favorable results.

Once you become accustomed to doing business with dealers and become confident in your wares, you may want to start selling direct to collectors. The best way to do this is to create a list of the items you have for sale and begin advertising its availability. Start out with classified ads.

When creating your list, make sure each description is clear on what you are selling and give attribution numbers and grades for each coin. Make sure you offer a liberal return policy and fair postage rates. Nothing turns off a prospective customer more than seeing a dealer attempting to gouge the buyer with excessive postage and handling charges and/or a short return policy. Offering seven to 14 days return privileges is reasonable but offering something as short as three days is not. $2 or $3 is reasonable for postage, $7 is not.

I suggest you ask at least $1 for your list as this tends to weed out those who are just seeking a guide to use to price their own coins but have no real intent in buying anything from you.

You may also want to post your list on the Internet in the form of a web-page. You can then offer hard-copy versions of your list for a price and a free viewing of the list on the Internet.

Your third avenue for selling errors and varieties is through auction. In general, most of the coins you will find will not be of interest to the large auction houses that deal in coins valued in the thousands of dollars. However, there are at least two error-variety clubs currently offering auction services at modest cost that will handle just about all the significant variety coins that you want to sell. If the coin sells, you pay a commission, and if it doesn't, you simply pay the postage to have it returned to you. These club auctions also offer the distinct advantage of you having a qualified auctioneer quickly examine your coins to make sure they are what you say they are before going into auction. These folks will not do detailed examinations for you, nor will they attribute coins to their proper listing numbers, but they will kick back any improperly described or undesirable items rather then letting it go through auction. At that point, you have the option of reeducating yourself or seeking help from a qualified error-variety coin attributer.

If you really feel confident that you have checked and doubled checked your coins and that they are what you hope they are, then you may try other auctions where there may in fact be nobody there to double check your attributions. If you plan to send your coins in for professional certification (see the chapter on certification services), you can participate in Teletrade Auctions. This firm only auctions off certified coins. The trick here is to make sure you send your coins into certification services that attribute varieties on the holder. If they do not or if they only recognize a select few then you may be doing yourself a disservice sending the coins in to the wrong company only to get coins back graded but with no variety or error coin attributions. If you are not sure, call the company and ask.

On-line auctions are probably the fastest growing area being utilized to sell coins today. If you are confident your coins are attributed accurately and if you can scan images of your coins, try the on-line auctions like those offered by eBay or Yahoo. These can be excellent avenues to sell coins. We suggest you browse through other dealers' auctions and see how they set up their auctions and what image hosting services they use, etc., before venturing forth into this area. You'll quickly get the idea that there is plenty of help out there to set up nice looking auctions that will help sell your wares.

The authors of this book wish you luck!

WHERE TO START SELLING YOUR COINS

Use the locations below to get started in selling your coins. It may take some time to locate the appropriate location to sell your coin, but will prove to be worth the effort.

Internet Auction Services
Registration is generally required but is normally at no-charge. Applicable fees will be determined by the auction service in accordance with the Terms of Agreement. If you do not own a computer, contact your local library, school, family member or friend.

YAHOO! AUCTIONS
http://auctions.yahoo.com/
Coins, Paper Money, & Stamps

EBAY ON-LINE AUCTIONS
www.ebay.com
Categories:Coins:errors

AMAZON.COM AUCTIONS
www.amazon.com
auctions

TELETRADE (Available on-line and through catalog)
www.teletrade.com
Teletrade
27 Main Street
Kingston, NY 12401-3853
Phone 845-339-2900
Fax 845-339-6279

Don't own a computer? No problem......
The clubs listed on the following page offer bi-monthly auctions. These auctions can be viewed on-line or through a catalog, generally offered at a small fee. Some may require club membership for participation in their auctions. For auction guidelines, contact the respective club (be sure to include a SASE).

National Collectors' Association of Die Doubling (NCADD)
http://www.ncadd.f2s.com/auction
John W. Bordner (President)
P.O. Box 15 Lykens, PA 17048-0015
jwb209@epix.net

Combined Organization of Numismatic Error Collectors of America (CONECA)
http://conecaonline.org/
or Write to:
Mike Bozovich
P. O. Box 878
Godfrey, IL 62035-0878 mkb@ezl.com

Try these methods as well.........

The addresses below are coin-related newspapers that offer classified ads, coin news and price guides. The classified ad section of these newspapers provide for a wide range of readers and potential buyers. To inquire about the classified ads, contact the Customer Service department for the respective publisher.

COINWORLD
Customer Service Department
P.O. Box 150
Sidney, OH 45365-0150
www.coinworld.com

NUMISMATIC NEWS
Customer Service Department
700 E. State St.
Iola, WI 54990
www.krause.com/coins/nn

A classified ad sample that you can even try in your local newspaper!

For Sale: 1969S Doubled Die Obverse, found in pocket change. $5,500.00.
Write with SASE to: John Doe, P.O. Box 12345, Anywhere, USA 12345

SOURCES FOR COIN INFORMATION

SPECIALTY COIN CLUBS

National Collectors Association of Die Doubling (NCADD), P.O. Box 15, Lykens, PA 17048-0015, jwb209@epix.net
http://geocites.com/ResearchTriangle/Facility/4968/NCADD.html

Combined Organization of Numismatic Error Collectors of America (CONECA,) 35 email: pfunny@telplus.net or visit
http://conecaonline.org/ http://conecaonline.org/

Yahoo! Clubs errorworld (On-line Internet Error Club)
http://clubs.yahoo.com/clubs/errorworld

PUBLICATIONS
(Weekly, Monthly or Bi-Monthly Publications)

Error and Variety Newsletter, (on-line only) Ken Potter, P.O. Box 760232 Lathrup Village, MI 48076-0232, E-mail: KPotter256@aol.com or visit www.koinpro.com

COINWORLD, P.O. Box 150, Sidney, OH 45365-0150

Numismatic News, 700 E. State St., Iola WI 54990

THE HUB, (NCADD) P.O. Box 15, Lykens, PA 17048-0015
http://geocites.com/ResearchTriangle/Facility/4968/NCADD.html

ERRORSCOPE, (CONECA) , email: pfunny@telplus.net or visit
http://conecaonline.org/

Error Trends Coin Magazine, P.O. Box 158, Oceanside, NY 11572-0158

Cherrypickers' News, P.O. Box 15487, Savannah, GA 31416-9280

COIN VERIFICATION AND ATTRIBUTION PROVIDERS

While general information on coins can be obtained from local coin dealers and clubs, reliable information on errors and varieties is not always as easily found. These services require the assistance of a professional who is well versed in this area of specialization.

The list of persons and companies below have all been found to be reliable in this area and come highly recommended. Prior to shipping any coins, you should always contact the location to receive shipping, packaging, return time and payment instructions. Many of the services will mail an information packet upon request that will contain all required information for submission. Sending a self-addressed stamped envelope will speed up the reply.

BRIAN ALLEN
rglerdude@hotmail.com

KEN POTTER
P.O. Box 760232
Lathrup Village, MI 48076-0232
kpotter256@aol.com
http://koinpro.tripod.com/index.htm

AMERICAN NUMISMATIC ASSOCIATION(ANA)
818 N. Cascade Ave.
Colorado Springs, CO 80903-3279
www.money.org

AMERICAN NUMISMATIC ASSOCIATION CERTIFICATION SERVICE (ANACS)
P.O. Box 7173
Dublin, OH 43017-0773
www.anacs.com

CoinWorld
Collectors Clearinghouse
P.O. Boc 150
Sidney, OH 45365-0150
http://www.coinworld.com/

COMBINED ORGANIZATION OF NUMISMATIC ERROR COLLECTORS ASSOCIATION (CONECA)
email: pfunny@telplus.net
http://conecaonline.org/

BILLY G. CRAWFORD
dievarieties@sc.rr.com

ERROR COIN TRENDS MAGAZINE
P.O. Box 158
Oceanside, NY 11572-0158
http://www.etcmmag.com/

NATIONAL COLLECTORS ASSOCIATION OF DIE DOUBLING (NCADD)
P.O. Box 15
Lykens, PA 17048-0015
jwb209@epix.net
http://geocites.com/ResearchTriangle/Facility/4968/NCADD.html

NUMISMATIC GUARANTEE CORPORATION (NGC)
P.O. Box 4776
Sarasota, FL 34230
http://www.ngccoin.com

PHOTO-CERTIFIED COIN INSTITUTE (PCI)
3952 Brainerd Road
Chattanooga, TN 37411
http://www.chattanooga.net/pci/index.html

PROFESSIONAL COIN GRADING SERVICE (PCGS)
P.O. Box 9458
Newport Beach, CA 92658
www.pcgs.com

SOVEREIGN ENTITY GRADING SERVICE (SEGS)
401 Chestnut St. Suite 103
Chattanooga, TN 37402
http://www.segscoins.com/

FRED WEINBERG
13611 Ventura Blvd
Encino, CA 91436
http://www.fredweinberg.com

NUMISMATIC NEWS
700 E. State St.
Iola WI 54990
http://www.krause.com/coins/nn

AMERICAN NUMISMATIC ASSOCIATION
MEMBERSHIP APPLICATION

YES, I want to be part of America's Coin Club. I understand that I will receive the Association's monthly magazine, The Numismatist; have access to 30,000 books in the world's largest numismatic lending library; will be eligible for discounts on numismatic books; and obtain dozens of other exclusive member benefits.

Name _____

Address _____

C/S/Z _____

Country _____Birth date _____

Enclosed is $35 (US funds) for a 1 year membership

Enclosed is $42 (US funds) for 1 year membership outside the US

Annual membership dues (with the exception of Associate membership) include $15 for a one-year subscription to The Numismatist.

To Join With a Credit Card:
CALL: 1-800-367-9723
FAX: 1-719-634-4085
EMAIL: anamem@money.org

Credit Card Account No. (all digits)/ Expiration Date
(MC, VISA, AmEx or Discover) OR RETURN APPLICATION WITH PAYMENT TO:

AMERICAN NUMISMATIC ASSOCIATION
818 NORTH CASCADE AVENUE
COLORADO SPRINGS, CO 80903-3279

I herewith make application for membership in the American Numismatic Association, subject to the bylaws of said Association. I also agree to abide by the Code of Ethics adopted by the Association.

Signature of Applicant/ Date

CONECA Membership Application

Today's Date: _____/_____/_____

Membership Type: _____ Regular/Annual Member - $25.00
                    _____ Young Numismatist (under 18) - $5.00

Mailing Options: _____ U.S. Bulk rate - No extra charge
                    _____ First Class or Foreign - $7.50 additional

Total: _____ Amount due

Name: _____

Address: _____

    City: _____State: _____

    Zip+Four Code: _____

Phone: _____

E-mail: _____

Recommended by: _____

Comments/Interests:

_____

_____

Send application and check/money order (payable to CONECA) to:
Paul Funaiole
35 Leavitt Lane
Glenburn, ME 04401-1013
pfunny@telplus.net

Your membership is subject to approval by the Membership Committee and subject to the rules and regulations set forth in the CONECA Constitution and By-Laws.

The National Collectors Association of Die Doubling
Membership Application

Name of Applicant_____

Address_____

City_____State: ____ Zip Code+Four_____—_____

Area Code and Phone Number (____)____-_____

E-mail (If Applicable) _____

*Regular Membership-$25 ___

Youth Membership (Through 17 Years of Age, With D.O.B and Parental Consent)-$10___

Date of Birth_____ Signature of Parent or Guardian_____

5 year Membership-$110 ___

Life Membership (After the First Year)-$450___ (Limited to 5% of regular membership)

Membership of Coin Clubs-$50 ___(Clubs will receive Two copies of the Newsletter)

Family Membership (Additional Family Members of a Regular Member**)____

**Number of Family Member(s)___x-$8=_____ (One Newsletter per Household)

*For Newsletter by First Class, U.S. Residents Add $9 Per Year for Postage. Canadian Residents Must Add $9 Per Year for Newsletter Postage. Other Countries Contact Us for Additional Postage Fees.

Total Enclosed $_____

Please Tell Us What Your Interest Are:
Doubled Dies____ Doubled Mint Marks____ Errors____ Other_____

I am interested in the Following Denominations
Cents____ Nickels____ Dimes____ Quarters____ Halves____ Dollars____ 50 States Quarters____ Errors____

Please indicate your level of coin experience:

_____

Make Check Payable To: *"NCADD"* and Mail To:
Brian Allen
P.O. Box 11081
Fayetteville, NC 28303
BrianWAllen@aol.com

You can visit the NCADD Website at:
http://geocites.com/ResearchTriangle/Facility/4968/NCADD.html

Membership is subject to review by the Board of Directors, NCADD's Rules and Regulation and Constitution.

THE MYTH ABOUT THE WHEAT CENT

Lincoln cents minted prior to 1959 with the old "wheat" reverse (or what are commonly referred to as "wheat-backs" or "wheaties") are hoarded by the American public by the billions. They frequently escape into circulation and are later found and tucked away as new-found treasures that the "lucky" discoverer is convinced is worth a fortune. Later they learn that their treasures are worth very little over face value.

The fact is, very few dates of the Lincoln cent with wheat reverse are worth much over two-cents. While there are a few key and semi-key dates that are worth significant premiums, the majority of these were removed from circulation decades before the hoards of common dates were assembled. Occasionally one of these keys is found in a bulk bag of wheat cents but that is a rarity as most bags have been searched several times before being sold off to dealers for further distribution in bag lots.

Do not expect to take a quantity of wheat cents into a dealer and have them checked individually for valuable pieces. It is your job to search through bulk lots that you may encounter to remove any pieces that may carry a premium — not the dealer's. Dealers will generally buy wheat cents at a percentage of retail and simply resell them without checking them for certain dates.

An example of a "clogged die" on a Lincoln Cent. This minor type of error is relatively common and worth 25c-50c.

Updated prices for coins listed in this book can be seen at our web-site: http://koinpro.tripod.com/Treasures.htm

MYTHS ABOUT THE BICENTENNIAL COINS

To commemorate the 200th Anniversary of American Independence, the United States released Bicentennial theme quarters, halves and dollars. These pieces were dual-dated 1776-1976 and were made in 1975 and 1976. Because they were minted for two years and because the anticipated demand was expected to be high, the mintages were extremely high. Furthermore, the pieces were withdrawn from circulation almost as quickly as they were minted by an eager public, convinced they would be worth something someday. The result is that virtually the entire mintage of these coins is being hoarded by an unknowing public as "treasures" to be cashed in at some point when they become "valuable."

The fact is, the supply continues to be extremely high due to hoarding. Thus the coins have minimal values over face, only in original uncirculated rolls. Loose pieces accumulated from circulation currently have no extra value and would be better deposited in a bank account to draw interest than to held for another 25 years waiting in vain for them to increase in value!

We do recommend, however, that you examine all of the 1976-D twenty-five cent pieces for the very elusive and expensive doubled obverse variety. Finding this particular quarter could bring you a very nice profit if you were lucky enough to have saved one! See the chapter on Washington quarter varieties for more details on this coin.

The 1975-1976 quarters are generally common stock and can be found in nice Uncirculated condition at most coin shops for $1-$2 and even purchased in original rolls. Circulated copies that are pulled from pocket change command NO value above 25c. We do recommend that you examine all of the 1976-D pieces for the very elusive and expensive Doubled Obverse. This particular quarter could bring you a very nice profit if you were to locate it!

ABOUT THE SUSAN B. ANTHONY DOLLAR

There is a misconception that suggests that since these coins were only produced for four years, (1979-1981 and 1999), and are not readily found in circulation that they must be "rare and valuable." Such is not the case. Like the Bicentennial coinage described above, the oft disdained Susan B. Anthony dollar has been minted in large quantities and has been the subject of hoard-

ing. They are still available at banks (when they come in) and are commonly encountered at the US Post Office as change from stamp vending machines found in the larger outlets. It should be noted that the 1981 issues were only minted for inclusion in government issues Mint sets sold to collectors. As a result, these are a bit scarce but still only command about $3.00 each. Since they were never released into circulation they are unlikely to be found there.

1943 WHEAT CENT MYTHS

This is the very rare and valuable copper cent of 1943.

COIN COURTESY: Steve Benson   *PHOTO COURTESY: Steve Benson*

By now everyone had heard of the 1943 "Steel" cent that was recently lost in circulation and reputed to be worth one-million dollars! WRONG! In fact, virtually all 1943 Lincoln cents were struck on zinc plated steel blanks due to a need to divert copper – a strategic wartime metal — from coinage to the manufacture of munitions. The mintages were relatively high and because the coins were "different" they were hoarded. As a result, they are not rare or particularly valuable. Values range from a few cents for average circulated grades to well under $50 even for the highest of certified uncirculated grades.

This is the common steel cent of 1943, only worth a few cents.

The confusion over the value of these cents stems from the existence of a few very rare "transitional" 1943 cents that were inadvertently struck on bronze blanks left over from 1942. However, while they are rare and expensive, even these do not approach anywhere near the one-million dollar mark that the general press has propagandized in recent years. The two highest grade specimens to hit the auction block in recent months (late 2000) traded at record prices of just over one-hundred-thousand dollars each. There are currently about 30 pieces known for all three of the Mints that were in operation that year.

It should be noted that this error is one of the most widely faked coins of all time! Thousands were plated for a magazine publisher that distributed them with a subscription offer as a novelty item back in the 1950s. Others have been likewise plated for distribution as novelty pieces or to defraud. Other fakes represent alterations of 1948 cents by shaving and reforming the 8 into a 3. The plated pieces are easily detected with a magnet. If they are a copper-plated fake they will be drawn by the magnet by the steel core. If they are genuine, they will not. If they are nonmagnetic, a careful inspection of the date is in order. If the date was altered into a 1943 from a 1948 cent (or maybe even a 1953 cent), the style of the date will differ from that of a 1943. Remember, to even qualify as a possible authentic 1943 bronze cent, it must be nonmagnetic and it must have the correct style of date. However, even passing these two tests does not guarantee the coin's authenticity; cast or even die-struck counterfeits are possible, so it is recommended that any piece suspected to be a genuine 1943 bronze cent be authenticated by a professional service.

MYTHS ABOUT TWO-HEADED AND OTHER MISMATCHED COINS

 A double-headed coin is actually an alteration made from two coins with the final product known as a "magician's coin." They can be purchased as a novelty item in "magic shops" or from ads in places like comic books for about $4 to $6 depending on the denomination involved. More recently they have become available from vendors on the Internet ranging from single coins to entire sets of double-headed or double-tailed coins. (Even exotic pieces that mate a Lincoln cent obverse with a Roosevelt dime reverse or a Washington quarter obverse with a Sacagawea dollar reverse are contrived in machine shops and sold as novelty items.)

After being used as gags for a time, the magician's coin frequently got spent as a regular coin by mistake. In short order it is found by somebody else who is convinced it is a rare Mint error. When told what it is by a qualified expert, the owner usually protests, suggesting that his coin is "different" — it was studied closely and there is no seam on the edge to suggest that two coins had their reverses (or obverses) filed down and glued together.

However, "magician's coins" are not made that way, and unless one knows what to look for, they are very difficult to detect. The place to look is not on the edge, but on the inside of the design rim on either side of the coin. This is because one side is comprised of a lathed out or hollowed out coin shell and the other side is made from a coin lathed around its circumference and reduced in thickness to fit snugly inside the shell. The resulting coin is virtually undetectable to the average observer, most of whom ignore the peculiar thud (rather than the familiar ring) the coin emits when dropped on a hard surface.

For the record, the Mint grinds "flats" of different sizes into the head of the shanks of dies that prevents the obverse and reverse dies to be set interchangeably — thus two obverses or reverses cannot be paired together as a unit to strike coins.

If there was ever a doubt as to the origin or how the "magician's coins" are made, I quote information that was sent to me in December of 1991 by one of the distributors of two- headed coins, BR Numismatics of Flushing Michigan.

Company spokesman, Bradley C. Regan describes his productions as follows:

"My Lucky Quarter Novelty Tokens are each handmade and fitted together, each one is machined out of two individual new quarters. The first half is hollowed out to a thickness of .031" and an inside diameter of .875." The second half has the outside diameter machined to .874" and is then machined to a thickness of .031". Each half is then deburred with a hone and bonded together with a drop of instant metal adhesive. I then put the Lucky Quarters in special packaging for resale. These Lucky Quarter Novelty Tokens are not a US Mint made product, needless to say, and are not sold as such. According to the US Treasury Department of Secret Service, these Lucky Quarters are legal to sell as long as it is done without fraudulent intent or if the coins are not used fraudulently."

Just prior to the publishing of this book, two authentic "Two-Tailed" Quarters were discovered in an old collection. How these errors could have occurred is a complete mystery. However, these authors believe that these are the only two authentic copies that will ever be found. Be very cautious of fakes! ....One authentic piece sold for over $80,000. See Chapter 14.

COMMON NOVELTIES

It is not uncommon to encounter "neat" looking coins that could easily be perceived as valuable at first glance. Throughout history, many novelty coins have been sold as souvenirs.

MYTHS ABOUT COINS WITH NO MINT MARKS

A news story emanating from the general press several years ago, reported upon a truly valuable error coin that was missing a "P" Mint mark when the die was put into service to strike coins. This was the 1982 No P Roosevelt dime listed in this book. The story led people to believe that all coins missing a Mint mark are valuable errors. This is not the case.

No Lincoln Cents have ever contained the "P" Mint mark. Pieces struck without the Mint mark usually represent Philadelphia strikes (though some have

been made at other Mints in limited quantities and all Denver issues were struck without a Mint mark for all denominations in 1965-1967). Furthermore, with one exception, all higher denominations minted in Philadelphia prior to 1980 were intentionally struck without a Mint mark. Only the wartime, silver alloy Jefferson nickels of 1942-1945 and the 1979-P Susan B. Anthony dollar of 1979 were minted with a P Mint mark prior to 1980. Just because the media puts something into print does not make it valid.

COMMON CURRENCY QUESTIONS

If a coin dealer "had a dollar" for every time someone asked "What is a Two-Dollar bill worth," most dealers could retire with only a couple of years of business behind them. The truth of the matter is that the small size series of $2 bills are fairly common and not difficult to locate. Small size $2 denominations were produced in 1928, 1953, 1963, 1976 and 1995. Values on $2 notes will range from $2-$7 for most years with 1928 being a more valuable year. The ultimate value of a $2 bill will depend on the condition, year, seal, and signature of the treasurer. Currency books can be found for under $10 at your local book store. If you are interested in $2 bills contact your banker; most banks can provide $2 at no additional premium.

SILVER CERTIFICATES

Yes, Silver Certificates are worth more than $1; however, as mentioned above the condition, signatures, date and now the state of issue will determine the value. The values of these notes can range from $1.25 to several hundred dollars. There are more specifics on Silver Certificates than we can describe in this book, so you may want to contact your local dealer or purchase a currency book. What we would like to emphasize here, is that none of these should be overlooked.

INTERESTED IN CURRENCY?

Although currency is not pocket change, we felt comfortable including a one-dollar note that could earn you a few more dollars with some time and hunting.

The "Web-Note" is a series of bills that were produced using a new "web-press" in 1995, that should have increased the Bureau of Printing and Engravings' proficiency and produced more one-dollar bills. After a short trial, the Bureau of Printing and Engravings abandoned the process and went back to the previous method of currency production.

The value of the "web-note" will vary with condition, date, treasure etc., generally "web-notes" are valued at $1.25- $5.00. When purchasing web-notes, dealers would like to purchase large numbers of web-notes, not individual pieces. We suggest to save 20-30 web-notes that you find and sell them to an interested dealer at $1.15-$1.25 each. Your local dealer may be able to assist you with more information on the value of these scarce notes.

HOW TO FIND A "WEB-NOTE"

To find a web-note simply look for the number on the back of the bill. Normal One-Dollar bills will have the number in the lower right corner.

NORMAL!

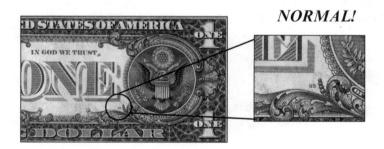

The photo below shows the location of the number on a web-note. Yes! That is all it takes to find one of these scarce bills.

WEB NOTE!

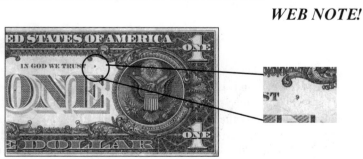

CIRCULATING SILVER COINAGE

With the exception of the Lincoln cent, all of our current designs, from the Jefferson nickel through the Kennedy half, have been struck in various alloys of silver. The Jefferson nickel was struck in an alloy containing 35% silver from 1942 through 1945, while dimes through halves were struck in 90% silver from

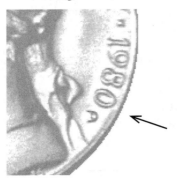

Mint mark location for NON-silver coinage from 1968-2000.

Mint mark location for Non-silver nickels dated 1938-1942 and 1946-1964.

their inceptions through pieces dated 1964. Kennedy halves made for circulation from 1965-1969 contained an alloy of 40% silver (pieces struck in 1970 were also 40% silver but only available in government issued collector sets, and are worth a considerable premium but are not apt to be found in circulation).

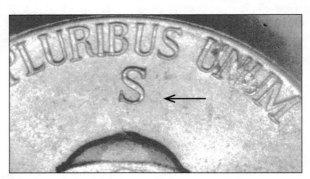

Silver Nickels Mint marks for 1942-1945.

Of all of these issues, the one you are most apt to find is the Kennedy half in 90% and 40% silver. The Kennedy half was a very special coin to many Americans in the 1960s and even later years and many were kept as mementoes to the fallen president. Even today the Kennedy half is hoarded for no particular reason other than it is seldom seen. Of course, most hoarders eventually cash in and it is not infrequent for rolls of half dollars to be taken to the bank and

Strike It Rich With Pocket Change

exchanged for cash. Because many folks forget that the first few issues were silver, they often get mixed in with the later "clad" date pieces. Even the earlier Franklin halves sometimes get mixed into these rolls.

While you may encounter such rolls at any time, the best time to look is just before and after Christmas when folks need extra cash to go shopping.

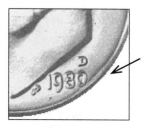

Mint mark location for Non-Silver dimes from 1968-2000.

Mint mark for silver dimes from 1946-1964.

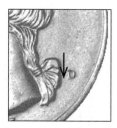

Mint mark position for non-silver quarters dated 1968-2000.

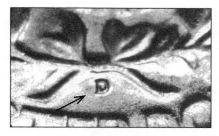

Mint mark location for silver quarters dated 1932-1964.

Mint mark location for the JFK Half Dollar from 1965-1970 on 40% silver planchets.

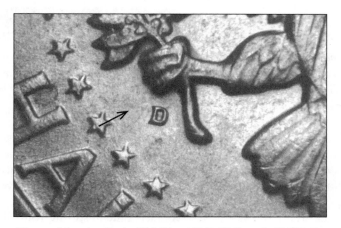

Mint mark location for the 90% Silver 1964D JF Kennedy Half-Dollar

"TISSUE OVERLAY" DETECTION OF SILVER COINS

Of all the methods to detect coins that are struck on the wrong metal for the year that it was designed to be struck on, this method is the quickest, easiest, and perhaps more accurate than a few of the others. This method is basically cost free and can be conducted with one coin or several coins at the same time. This method was developed by dealers as a means of aiding dealers in picking out silver coinage from large numbers of coins.

How? Simply lay the coins on a flat surface, lay a white tissue cloth directly over the coins, and then apply a light over the top.

What to look for? A silver or even partial silver coin will appear white in comparison to grayish-brown color of the normal circulation coinage. To assist you with getting started, look at a Nickel, Dime or Quarter from your pocket change under the tissue. The color difference between a normal coin and a silver coin will be easy to distinguish.

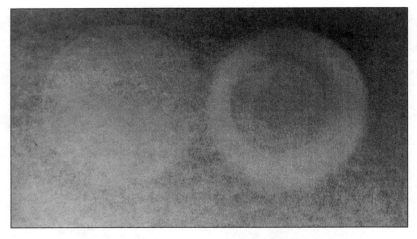

The image on the left is of a non-silver coin, notice the gray-brown tone. The image on the right is a large silver coin with a non-silver dime lying directly on top. The comparison photo on the right shows the difference in colors as they appear through the tissue cloth.

Use this test to assist you with finding the very valuable pocket change that was errantly struck (such as the 1965 Washington Quarter) on a silver blank. Even while the "tissue overlay" is quick and easy, you will still need to conduct a weight and metal composition test in the event you find a possible error coin struck on a silver blank.

You can also use this test to save yourself time in sorting your silver coins from normal coins.

SILVER VALUE CONVERSION

It pays to know the years of silver coinage. Many turn up in change everyday. This is one aspect of treasure hunting that the condition of the coin will have little to no effect on the value of the coin, for the price is primarily based off the metal content not the grade or any particular error contained on the coin. We detailed the metal compositions of each denomination at the beginning of each chapter but will detail only the years of silver coinage here, with the exact weight of silver expressed in ounces. By using the exact weight of silver expressed in ounces you can multiply the current U.S. market value of silver by the silver content and determine the pure silver value of the coin.

The price of U.S. silver can rise or fall daily so it is important to look at the current value of the day prior to selling any silver coins. You can get the current silver values from the local newspaper, your bank or *http://collectors.com/coins/index.html*. The value of your coin may only change minimally with the fluctuating silver prices, but it could add greatly to the overall sell of a large quantity of coins.

U.S. COINAGE ONLY
Jefferson Nickel silver coins from 1942-1945, *Net silver: 0.05626 ounces*
Roosevelt Dimes, silver coins from 1946-1964, *Net silver: 0.07234 ounces*
Washington Quarter, silver coins from 1932-1964, *Net silver 0.18084 ounces*
Kennedy Half-Dollars, 90% silver during 1964, *Net silver 0.36167 ounces*
Kennedy Half-Dollars, 40% silver from 1965-1970, *Net silver 0.1479 ounces*

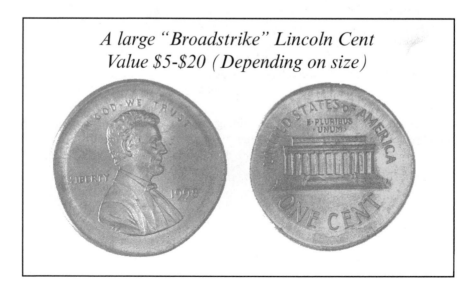

A large "Broadstrike" Lincoln Cent
Value $5-$20 (Depending on size)

1999-2009 "50-STATES" QUARTER PROGRAM

In 1999 the U.S. Mint began releasing a series of commemorative quarters representing each of the 50 states. The program calls for the release of five different states quarters per year for a duration of ten years with each state released in the order in which it became a member of the Union.

The states quarter program has been well received by both the general public and the numismatic community (coin collectors) and is expected to add millions of new collectors to the ranks.

In response, dealers have seized upon this opportunity to market a wide array of numismatic products to aid in the storage and collecting of these quarters.

While none of these quarters are rare, with mintages well into the hundreds of millions, so many collectors are assembling them into sets that "shortages" of some of the earlier issues have already developed. Rolls of $10 face value 1999 Delaware, Pennsylvania and New Jersey peaked at $50 per roll at one point with current levels still well over $23.00.

What we suggest is that you try obtaining original "bank-wrapped" rolls from your financial institution and holding them for a short period to see if they increase in value. Most probably will not increase dramatically, but you never know.

50 States Quarters Release Dates
(In order of release)

1999
Delaware Dec-07-1787
Pennsylvania Dec-12-1787
New Jersey Dec-18-1787
Georgia Jan-02-1788
Connecticut Jan-09-1788

2000
Massachusetts Feb-06-1788
Maryland Apr-28-1788
South Carolina May-23-1788
New Hampshire Jun-21-1788
Virginia Jun-25-1788

2001
New York Jul-26-1788
North Carolina Nov-21-1789
Rhode Island May-29-1790
Vermont Mar-04-1791
Kentucky Jun-01-1792

2002
Tennessee Jun-01-1796
Ohio Feb-19-1803
Louisiana Apr-30-1812
Indiana Dec-11-1816
Mississippi Dec-10-1817

2003
Illinois Dec-03-1818
Alabama Dec-14-1819
Maine Mar-15-1820
Missouri Aug-10-1821
Arkansas Jun-15-1836

2004
Michigan Jan-26-1837
Florida Mar-03-1845
Texas Dec-29-1845
Iowa Dec-28-1846
Wisconsin May-29-1848

2005
California Sep-09-1850
Minnesota May-11-1858
Oregon Feb-14-1859
Kansas Jan-29-1861
West Virginia Jun-20-1863

2006
Nevada Oct-31-1864
Nebraska Mar-01-1867
Colorado Aug-01-1876
North Dakota Nov-02-1889
South Dakota Nov-02-1889

2007
Montana Nov-08-1889
Washington Nov-11-1889
Idaho Jul-03-1890
Wyoming Jul-10-1890
Utah Jan-04-1896

2008
Oklahoma Nov-16-1907
New Mexico Jan-06-1912
Arizona Feb-14-1912
Alaska Jan-03-1959
Hawaii Aug-21-1959

RECOMMENDED COIN BOOKS

The books listed below are all available from Ken Potter. If you have an interest in learning more about the thousands of valuable coins that can be found in your pocket change, contact this publisher for the best book to suit your needs.

There are hundreds of other coin books that cover other denominations, foreign and obsolete coins. View the web-site listed at the end of this section to view the possibilities.

BOOKS

The Official Price Guide to Mint Errors - 6th Edition by Alan Herbert. This all new edition of Alan Herbert's Official Price Guide To Mint Errors is **entirely rewritten and expanded to over 400 pages!** With this sixth edition, Herbert brings us over 25 year of his expertise in this aspect of hobby! The book contains illustrated chapters on most error and variety types with general pricing information on all. Just about anything you could possibly want to know about the minting process and how error coins are produced can be found within the pages of this book! Note: I am particularly proud (and more importantly — consider myself honored) to have been asked to write the Foreword to this book and to have supplied five of the six photos used on the front cover! I'd like to extend a big "Thank You!" to Alan Herbert for the honor. This book could have easily been printed on more expensive stock, with hard-covers and a slightly larger font size (to make it span over 500 pages), and offered at triple the price! Instead, Herbert chose to have it produced on more economical stock with soft covers by one of the big book publishers resulting in a price level anybody can afford! $14.95

The Cherrypickers' Guide To Rare Die Varieties, 4th Edition - Volume 1, by Bill Fivaz & J.T. Stanton. It's finally here! This long-awaited book covers important die varieties known on United States coins from the Half Cent through Jefferson Nickels (the balance of denominations will be covered in the 4th Edition — Volume 2 due out in the Fall of 2001). It spans 422 pages with well over one-thousand photos. It contains important information including the value of the coins, rarity, interest factors, cross reference listing numbers and a description of where to best view the variety. It also contains important chapters on the Minting Process, Other Forms of Doubling and the Classification of Doubled dies. Spiral Bound. Regular Price $34.95, Our price $29.95

Error-Variety News Classics - Book-1 — contains reprints of all articles from the first two years of John Wexler & Robert Wilharm's "Error-Variety News." Hours of interesting and educational reading! You will find feature articles and regular columns by some of the hobby's best error-variety coin authors. You will meet many of the people who helped build this hobby to where it is today, and you will read all about hundreds of new discoveries as they were originally reported upon. You will tour the world's Mints in Alan Herbert's, *Mints and Minting* column and get a chuckle out of Sam P. Roden's monthly cartoon! The Wexler/Wilharm issues feature a stable of outstanding authors like Alan Herbert, Delma K. Romines, Robert Larkin, Bill Fivaz, Steven Gray, Robert Wilharm, Margaret Wilharm, David Camire, Ricky Morse, David E. Van Gelder, Herbert Hicks, Tom Miller, Ken Potter, Jeffrey Daniher, David Crenshaw, Steven Ritter, Harrington E. Manville and, of course, John Wexler (who - believe it or not - also wrote about planchet and striking errors back in those days!). Book-1 represents all 20 issues of EVN from Volume 1 through Volume 2. Every article and every front cover has been published as originally presented. All dealer or club ads that appear in multiple issues without changes are included on their first-time-of-appearance. This allows new collectors in the field an opportunity to learn about the evolution of the hobby and who's who. These reprint compilations were produced with the newest state-of-the-art copy technology that results in extremely high-quality imagery, virtually equal to or better than the originals. The first volume is over 220 pages in the large 8-1/2 x 11" format and spiral bound. $24.95

Error-Variety News Classics - Book-2 — Contains reprints of all articles from the large size issues of John Wexler & Robert Wilharm's "Error-Variety News," Vol.3 - Vol.4 (19 issues in all). Hours of interesting and educational reading! Over 250 8-1/2 x 11" pages; spiral bound. $24.95

The Encyclopedia of Doubled Dies - Vol.1 & Vol.2 Combined, Wexler. **Latest reprint with advanced photo reproduction technology** (excellent reproduction of all photos that are superior to the originals!) Spiral bound $24.95

An Indexed Guide Book Of Silver Art Bars Long out of print and difficult to find, this is the 5th edition of *An Indexed Guide Book Of Silver Art Bars!* It was published by J Archie Kidd and edited by Steve M. Rood in 1991 and contains over 3,700 photos and listings for over 6,000 art bars, varieties, errors, and cancelled dies. Over 350 8-1/2 x 11" pages. It offers prices and mintage figures (when known) and other historical information that a collector of these miniature pieces of art may want to know. This book is highly sought after and bears a cover price of $29.95

Revised 1993 Supplement to the 5th Edition of An Indexed Guide Book Of Silver Art Bars. Lists over 500 Art Bars, Varieties, Errors and Cancelled Dies. Over 450 Photos! This is the long out of print and difficult to find supplement to the 5th edition of *An Indexed Guide Book Of Silver Art Bars.* It was limited to just 500 numbered copies. It gives mintages and a rarity and price guide. It also includes revisions (corrections, etc.) to the 5th edition. This book is highly sought after and bears a cover price of $14.95

Walter Breen's Complete Encyclopedia of U.S. and Colonial Coins (754 pgs.!!) **Everybody should own this massive textbook!** Regular Price $135.00, Our price $110.00

Treasure Hunting Walking Liberty Half Dollars by Kevin Flynn and Brian Raines. 122 pages, large 8-1/2 x 11" format. Chock full of doubled dies and RPM's plus regular sections that Flynn typically includes in all the books he works on. Regular price $29.95, Our Price $24.95

The Authoritative Reference On Roosevelt Dimes. Kevin Flynn's latest book in his "Authoritative" series. As usual — chock full of doubled dies, RPM's and OMM's + his normal chapters on the history of the series, etc.; 182, 8-1/2x11" pages, soft cover. Regular Price $32.95, Our Price $24.95

A Guide To The 1879-S Reverse Of 1878 Morgan Silver Dollars by David T. Wang. 54, 8-1/2x11" pages, soft cover. Small in size but highly specialized and fully illustrated, and well worth every cent! $24.95

Top 50 Peace Dollar Varieties Text by Jeff Oxman & Dr. David Close, Photos by Bill Fivaz & Dr. David Close. This 70 page book is the natural follow-up to the "Top 100 VAM Keys," an extremely successful book with a focus on Morgan Dollars, published in 1997 by Jeff Oxman and Michael S. Fey, Ph.D. This one brings the VAM enthusiast the Top 50 varieties on the Peace Silver Dollar that are of greatest interest to VAM collector! Published on high-quality glossy paper replete with several hundred sharp photomicrographs detailing the diagnostics of each variety. Large 8-1/2" x 11" format. $29.95

Standing Liberty Quarters - 3rd Edition, Kline $24.95

The RPM Book 1st edition, Wexler/Miller. If you are just starting out in variety collecting and want to start somewhere at a small cost — this is one of the books to start with. While the book is an older one (published in 1983) it is still the only book out there that covers Repunched Mint Marks and Over Mint Marks on all denominations and can still boast being about 85% complete in the area of Lincoln cents plus offering listings for all the other denominations — many of which have not appeared anywhere else in print. 296 pages soft cover. A super bargain at $14.95

The RPM Book - Lincoln Cents 2nd edition, Wiles (new and updated — covers all the Lincoln cents) Regular $34.95, Our Price $29.95

The Lincoln Cent Doubled Die, Wexler (Stanton Reprint of this classic) $18.95

The Jefferson Nickel RPM Book - An Attribution and Pricing Guide by James Wiles, Ph.D. This is one of the most anticipated books of the past few years. Wiles, CONECA's 20th Century U.S. die variety attribution specialist, has illustrated all of the known Jefferson nickel repunched mint marks and over mint marks, listed important information, and assigned values to all varieties listed. This is a must for the variety enthusiast and sure to be a best seller for those in search of varieties on this series! Regular $29.95 Our Price $24.95

Walter Breen's Encyclopedia of United States Half Cents 1793-1857 Large 8-1/2 x 11" format; more than 500 pages including color plates! Heavily illustrated throughout! A must for every numismatist that has an interest in this series or its varieties! Hardbound $57.00

Cameo And Brilliant Proof Coinage Of The 1950 To 1970 Era by Rick Jerry Tomaska. A noted pioneer and authority in a field considered by many to be one of the last great frontiers in U.S. Numismatics, Tomaska explains all the important facts of this specialized area. Learn the difference between Ultra Heavy Cameo, Heavy Cameo, Moderate Cameo, Light Cameo and Brilliant Proof coins by viewing the lavishly illustrated pages of every denomination, learn which dates are common, and which dates are scarce. Hardcover! (See his book on Franklin Halves also offered for sale in elsewhere!) 193 pages, 8-1/2 x 11" size format. List price is $39.00. Our price $34.95

The Complete Guide To Certified Barber Coinage by David & John Feigenbaum 145 pages 11 x 8-1/2" format. $25.00

The Comprehensive Catalog And Encyclopedia Of Morgan & Peace Dollars, (The VAM Book), by Leroy C. Van Allen & George Mallis This is the updated 4th edition of the standard textbook on Morgan & Peace dollars and their varieties. Within its over 500, 8-1/2" x 11" pages you will find a date-by-date analysis of every issue including general striking characteristics, expected luster, comments on proof-like strikes, how the coins were handled and, of course, a detailed and fully illustrated listing of thousands of thousands of significant die varieties! There are also chapters on Investing in Silver Dollars, The History of the Silver Dollar, How they Were Minted, Grading Dollars, The GSA Sales, The Redfield Hoard, Detecting Counterfeits, Storage & Preservation, Proof-like Coins, and Photographing Silver Dollars. This massive textbook retails at $79.95 in soft cover. Our price $69.95

The Complete Guide To Buffalo Nickels — 2nd edition by David Lange, This is the long awaited second edition; the first was a sellout. Dave Lange knows the series better than virtually any other numismatist and freely shares his knowledge of this popular series. The detailed text is highly educational and informational, and combined with the detailed photos makes a wonderful reference. 8.5" x 11" page size, over 200 pages, hard bound only. Don't delay - order today! $36.95

Joja Jemz Reprints by Bill Fivaz & J. T. Stanton. A compilation book of all of their popular fixed price list catalogs issued from 1987-1992. 696 pages and thousands of photos! A true classic for the true collector! $35.00

The Cherrypickers' Pocket Guide - The Top 150 Rare Die Varieties by Bill Fivaz & J.T. Stanton **Temporarily Sold Out**

The Comprehensive Encyclopedia of United States Liberty Seated Quarters by Larry Briggs List $39.95 $35.00

Treasure Hunting Mercury Dimes by John Wexler and Kevin Flynn — A fantastic book covering a sizeable number of Doubled Dies and Repunched Mint Marks — 120 pages, 8-1/2 x 11", over 350 photos. Prices for all varieties are covered. List $29.95. Our Price $24.95

The Complete Guide To Franklin Half Dollars by Rick Tomaska $19.95

Longacre's Two-Cent Piece - 1864 Attribution Guide by Frank Leone $22.50

The Authoritative Reference on Three Cent Nickels by Edward Fletcher and Kevin Flynn. The only reference available on the subject of Three Cent Nickels and their varieties! 155 pages, 8-1/2 x 11", over 250 photos! Prices for all varieties! List price $37.95. Our price 29.95

The 1878 Morgan Dollar 8-TF Attribution System by Les Hardnett & Jeff Oxamn **Temporarily Sold Out**

The 1878 Morgan Dollar 7/8-TF Attribution System by Les Hardnett & Jeff Oxamn **Temporarily Sold Out**

Treasure Hunting Liberty Head Nickels by Kevin Flynn and Bill Van Note — A fantastic book covering a sizeable number of Doubled Dies, Misplaced Dates and Repunched Dates — 130 pages, 8-1/2 x 11", over 390 photos. Prices for all varieties are covered. List $29.95. Our Price $24.95

The Best of the Washington Quarter Doubled Dies by John Wexler & Kevin Flynn. Over 186 8-1/2 x 11" pages; spiral bound. (Regular $29.95) Our price $24.95

The Washington Quarter Dollar Book - An Attribution and Pricing Guide - Vol. 1 1932-1941 by James Wiles. 250 pages of Doubled Die and Repunched Mint Marks! Every variety is priced and illustrated! Regular Price $40.00, Our Price $32.95

The Washington Quarter Dollar Book - An Attribution and Pricing Guide - Vol. 2 1942-1944 by James Wiles. 250 pages of Doubled Die and Repunched Mint Marks! Every variety is priced and illustrated! Regular Price $40.00, Our price $32.95

CONECA's Lincoln Cent RPM Price Guide, Mike Ellis $5.00

The Complete Price Guide and Cross Reference to Lincoln Cent Mint Mark Varieties, Brian Allen/John Wexler. Few photos but provides a cross index for Wexler and CONECA numbers; prices for circulated and uncirculated grades. Hardcover $45; soft cover $17.95

The Standard Guide To The Lincoln Cent - Fourth Edition Dr. Sol Taylor. A date by date analysis. $24.95

The Complete Guide To Lincoln Cents by David W. Lange. This is by far one of the best books available on the Lincoln Cent. David Lange is one of the premier authors today. Now available is the second printing (1999) with greatly improved photographs. There is no other reference on the subject that matches this work. 364 pages, 8.5" x 11", soft bound. $44.95

Flying Eagle, Indian Cent, Two Cent, Three Cent Doubled Dies by Kevin Flynn. 174 pages chock full of the most up-to-date information you need to keep abreast of the doubled dies on these series. Regular price $39.95, our price $32.00

Treasure Hunting Buffalo Nickels John Wexler/Ron Pope/Kevin Flynn. A heavily illustrated guide to Buffalo nickel varieties. Regular Price $29.94, Our price $24.95

Bill Fivaz's Counterfeit Detection Guide A neat little 52 page, pocket-size guide, detailing the diagnostics to look for on the genuine examples of many of the modern key dates. Every coin or variety illustrated! $10.00

Helpful Hints For Enjoying Coin Collecting by Bill Fivaz. A really neat introduction to numismatics! Covers: "The do's and don'ts of Coin Collecting," coin cleaning, grading, coin storage, coin conventions, tips on mailing coins, the minting process (by J.T. Stanton), numismatic terms and definitions, commonly used numismatic acronyms, recommended books and publications, joining specialty clubs, and much, much more on getting started in this fascinating hobby! $15.95

The Top 100 Morgan Dollar Varieties: The VAM Keys , Fey & Oxman. SB in leatherette cover $24.50

Detecting Counterfeit Gold Coins by Lonesome John Devine. This is the one and only — the original — Detecting Counterfeit Gold Coins by Lonesome John Devine! Tens of thousands of counterfeits exist on the popular coin types now being placed in portfolios every day! With a focus on the universally popular subject of counterfeit gold coins, Devine examines the diagnostics of many individual U.S. and foreign coins; numerous dates of

U.S. $1, $2-1/2, $3, $5, $10 & $20 gold coins are explored, the Canadian 1967 $20 gold, British Sovereigns, French, Netherlands, Russian, Mexican, Swiss, and other counterfeits are fully examined and illustrated by Devine's world renowned photography. You'll learn more here about the diagnostic features found on counterfeit gold than in any other book ever written on the subject! We Are The Exclusive Distributor Of This Book. They are new and sealed in plastic. $14.95

The CONECA Attribution Guide to the Kennedy Half Dollar (Varieties), James Wiles. Over 300 8-1/2 x 11" pages; 1400+ photos and prices for over 200 varieties. Spiral bound for easy use at no extra charge! List price $40 - Our special price $34.95

Morgan Dollar Overdates, Over Mintmarks, Misplaced Dates, and Clashed E Reverses by Kevin Flynn, a neat little 120 page book discussing, illustrating and pricing all the known varieties within the focus of the book. Refutes several of the long "established" OMMs and ODs with supportive analysis and overlays! Regular $19.95 - Sale price $17.95

The Comprehensive Catalog and Encyclopedia of Morgan & Peace Dollars (The VAM Book) - 4th Edition, Van Allen & Mallis. Massive textbook on silver dollar varieties! More than 500 large format pages! Soft cover $79.95

The Authoritative Reference on Eisenhower Dollars by John Wexler, Bill Crawford and Kevin Flynn. Over 200 pages replete with hundreds of photographs of all known varieties; pricing, a history of the series, grading and other interesting facts make this the most comprehensive effort on the series to date! $38.95

The Quick Reference to the Top Lincoln Cent Die Varieties by Wagnon, Peterson, Flynn $24.95

Treasure Hunting in the Flying Eagle and Indian Head Cent Series (pocket size book) by Kevin Flynn $19.95

A Quick Reference to the Top Misplaced Dates (pocket size book) by Kevin Flynn $19.95

Two Dates Are Better Than One - A Collector's Guide to Misplaced Dates, Kevin Flynn. Massive 512 pages!   Regular - $54.95,   Our price $35.00

Getting Your Two Cents Worth by Kevin Flynn. A Guide To 2c Die Varieties. List - $19.95 $12.95

The Complete Guide To Liberty Seated Half Dimes, Al Blyth (list $36) $29.00

The Complete Guide To Liberty Seated Dimes, Brian Greer (list $36) $29.00

The Complete Guide To Washington Quarters by John Feigenbaum hardcover $15.00

The Complete Guide To Shield and Liberty Nickels by Peters & Mohon (list $34.95) $25.00

The Design Cud, Marvin and Margolis. A Mint copy of this 1979 classic collectors item $10.95

Flying Eagle and Indian Cent Die Varieties by Steve & Flynn — 230 pages. This book covers many newer varieties not found in the now out-of-print Snow book. Regular $44.95 Sale $32.95

The Shield Five Cent Series - Varieties Fletcher. A truly great book full of photos! (Lists at $37) $29.95

ANA Certification Service Counterfeit Detection - Vol.1&2 $19.95

Striking Impressions - The Royal Canadian Mint & Coinage Haxby. A beautiful 300+ page textbook on the history of Canadian coinage and The Royal Canadian Mint. **More than 425 illustrations!** Originally sold at about $25 CN, Our price $14.95

The Variety Collectors' Listing To World Doubled Dies, Unillustrated listing to 620 varieties listed by Lou Coles Sale Price! $4.95

U.S. Copper Coins - An Action Guide for the Collector and Investor by Q. David Bowers $9.95

U.S. 3c and 5c Pieces - An Action Guide for the Collector and Investor by Q. David Bowers $9.95

U.S. 10c to 50c Pieces - An Action Guide for the Collector and Investor by Q. David Bowers $9.95

U.S. Coin Designs - An Action Guide for the Collector and Investor by Q. David Bowers $9.95

Variety Coin Center Error Catalog 3rd (1981 or 1982) edition, Neil Osena $4.00

HOW TO ORDER YOUR NEXT COIN BOOK

Terms of Sale: Satisfaction guaranteed! 14 days return privileges for items in original untampered holders — no questions asked. All checks must clear bank. Unless otherwise noted, please add $2.50 for postage/handling and insurance on all coin orders (including art bars, medals, rounds, defaced coinage dies and hobby memorabilia); add $2.50 for the first book ordered plus $1 per book thereafter (not to exceed $4.50), add $2.50 to all supply orders. Coin orders exceeding $200 shipped postpaid if paid for in cash (check or money order). Any book order exceeding $150 shipped postpaid if paid in cash (check or money order). Foreign orders cost extra — please contact me for the amount due at the time of your order. Books are shipped "Special 4th Class" unless other arrangements are made. No COD orders accepted. Due to market fluctuations, all prices are subject to change without notice. We reserve the right to not sell items at prices that are the result of typographical error. Make checks and money orders payable to and send to: Ken Potter P.O. Box 760232 Lathrup Village, MI 48076-0232 (313)255-8907 E-mail: KPotter256@aol.com or visit Ken Potter's Web-site at http://koinpro.tripod.com/books.htm

Updated prices for coins listed in this book can be seen at our web-site: http://koinpro.tripod.com/Treasures.htm

---

COIN SUPPLIES

Most coin dealers offer a wide selection of coin supplies, if you cannot locate what you need in your local area, there are several options available.

Use of the internet with "searches" of COIN, COIN SUPPLIES, or NUMISMATICS will assist you with locating one of the numerous suppliers of coin related materials. If you do not feel comfortable with using the internet or do not have a computer, contact your local coin dealer, one of the authors, or the publisher of this book.

Strike It Rich With Pocket Change

COIN TERMS AND DEFINITIONS

When conversing with dealers or coin collectors you may be required to understand a limited amount of coin terminology. Although this listing of coin terms is not all conclusive it should assist with questions that you may have concerning the material used in this book and avoid confusion when trying to convey the details of a particular coin.

"D"- The Mint mark representing coins struck at the Denver Mint (and gold coins struck at Dahlonega from 1838-1861).

"S"- The Mint mark representing coins struck at the San Francisco Mint.

"P"- The Mint mark representing coins struck in the Philadelphia Mint.

Alloy — A combination of two or more metals fused together in the molten state. For example: Bronze is an alloy of copper, tin and zinc.

Alteration – A coin that has been changed or altered to appear other than normal, with or without intent. Alterations usually represent pieces modified for jewelry or as novelty items but also include items altered with the intent to defraud. Double-headed magician's coins and cutout coin jewelry are examples of jewelry or novelty items. A 1944-D cent with the first 4 shaved into a 1 to appear as a rare 1914-D is an example of coin altered to defraud.

American Numismatic Association (ANA) – The world's foremost organization promoting numismatic education. Open to dealers, collectors, and researchers.

BIE — Reference given to a die break that occurs between the letters of B and E of LIBERTY on Lincoln cents when it takes on the appearance of an I and spells "BIE."

Blank — The disc of metal that will be processed further to have its edge raised, (at which point it is referred to as a planchet), and then struck into a coin. See Planchet.

Brass - An alloy of copper and zinc.

BREEN # — Reference numbers assigned to individual coins by date, Mint mark and type, (and some varieties), in Walter Breen's Complete Encyclopedia of U.S. & Colonial Coins.

Bronze – An alloy of copper, tin, and zinc.

Business Strike — A coin intended for circulation or public use or one struck in that manner.

Central Design – The main theme of a coin's design. For example, the portrait of John F. Kennedy is the central design on the obverse of the Kennedy half dollar, while the eagle is the central theme on its reverse.

Cherrypick — To find or purchase a rare variety that is unknowingly offered as a more common type.

Circulated — The presence of wear on a coin from circulation.

COIN TERMS AND DEFINITIONS CONTINUED

Clad – A planchet comprised of several layers of various metals bonded together into a single unit. Our current dimes through halves are clad coins comprised of a core of pure copper and layers of copper-nickel (75% copper and 25% nickel) bonded to either side.

Combined Organization of Numismatic Collectors of America (CONECA) — An organization dedicated to the study and education of error and variety coins.

Collar – The die that encircles the planchet at the time of striking. It restrains the outward flow of metal to assure the coin's round shape is maintained and it forms the reeded edge on coins that bear that device. This often overlooked die can also be the subject of die varieties and errors.

Collar Clash – See Die Clash.

Copper-Nickel — An alloy of copper and nickel.

Counterfeit – An unauthorized coin, struck, cast or otherwise created to pass as a genuine coin.

Cross Referencing — Providing listing numbers assigned outside of the body of work in which they are given, to aid the reader in finding more information on that variety in other works.

Cud – See "Major Die Break."

Designer — Person who creates the design used for a coin, medal or token.

Devices — The elements that make up a design. The "Central Design," stars, lettering and date are all "devices."

Die – A cylindrical bar of steel that has the design of a coin impressed into it incuse and which is used to strike coins.

Die Blank — A cylindrical-shaped piece of steel used to make dies and hubs.

Die Chip — A small, irregular cavity on the die resulting from a small chip. This results in a small raised area on the coin.

Die Clash (Die Clash Marks) — Marks on either or both dies that are the result of a planchet failing to enter the striking chamber and the dies smashing or "clashing" into each other. An upper die may also strike the edge of a collar resulting in the so-called "double rim" or on coins with reeding – evidence of reeding damage on the rim. Clash marks are very common and unless very strong, not normally worth premiums.

Die Crack — A split or crack in the face of a die, resulting in a raised, irregular, ridge on a coin.

Die Gouge – A raised area on the die that is the result of damage caused by a gouging action from engravers tools, ejection mechanisms, awls, or anything that results in a gouge in a die.

Die Life — The length of time a die remains in use, generally measured by the number of coins produced before being retired. Usually reported as estimates based on the average die life for a particular denomination in a given year or era.

Die Making Process — The entire process leading up to and including the making of a die. This includes the production of master tools, lathing operations, hubbing, heat treat, polishing and other finishing operations leading up to a usable die.

Die Marker – Any identifiable mark on a die that helps to identify or isolate it from others; usually in the form of die scratches, cracks, chips, etc., that are associated with a particular variety.

Die Scratch – Fine lines scratched into a die; usually the result of abrasives used to clean up or dress-out dies such as wire brushes, stones, aluminum oxide cloth, etc., or from contact with a sharp instrument. These lines will be raised on the coin.

Die Stage — Designates changes in the die such as die chips, scratches, cracks, clashes, etc. Usually documented in the order in which they occur by letters appended to listing numbers.

Die State — Describes the age of a die based on a variety of diagnostics including: sharpness of devices, die flow lines and die deterioration. Ranges from "very early die state (VEDS) to "very late die state" (VLDS).

Die Variety – Any variation in a coin's design, resulting from an intentional change or mishap during its production or use. The term is generally restricted to variations that are considered "collectable."

Double Denomination – A coin that has been struck by the dies of two different denominations such as a Roosevelt dime that has been struck a second time by Lincoln cent dies.

Doubled Die Obverse or DDO (Hub Doubled Die) – Refers to a coin struck with an obverse die that was doubled during its production via the hubbing process. See the chapter on doubling.

Doubled Die Reverse or DDR (Hub Doubled Die) – Refers to a coin struck with a reverse die that was doubled during its production via the hubbing process. See the chapter on doubling.

Dual Mint Mark (DMM) — A relative of the OMM, the DMM refers to a coin with two different and completely separate Mint marks. See the 1980D&S.

Early Die State (EDS) — Condition of the die shortly after it begins to show indications use. See Die State.

Engraver — Person or machine that engraves or touches up dies.

Field — The area of the obverse or reverse that contains no design; background. It may be textured or smooth.

Error – Loosely defined as any coin struck on a defective planchet or struck with dies containing an error or mechanically mis-struck in error or a combination of the above.

Metal Flow Lines – Radiating lines on the surface of a die or coin created by the natural outward flow of metal eroding the die. Metal flow lines become progressively heavier as the die sees use. These lines are often removed (or partially removed) several times during the life of a die via die dressings with abrasives.

COIN TERMS AND DEFINITIONS CONTINUED

Specks — Small carbon spots (more often than not on copper coins) often caused by moisture.

Grade — The condition of a coin based on many factors including: wear (for circulated coins), luster, marks, strike, color, and eye appeal.

High Point — Highest point of detail on a coin. This is normally the first area to show signs of wear.

Incuse – Refers to a sunken design that is lower than the surface of the field or other area in which is found. Opposite of "relief" or "raised."

Lamination — The layering, peeling or flaking of metal on a coin due to trapped slag, gases or other impurities being trapped in the metal at the time the ingots were formed (from which the coinage strip was made).

Legend — The inscription(s) other than the date and denomination found on a coin.

Major Die Break (Cud) – A broken die involving a piece that breaks from the shank and extends inward into the design. The result is often what appears to be a blob of raised metal in the area where the broken chunk of die fell out and a corresponding area of weakness on the side opposite the cud. Cud is a nickname taken from the appearance of the blob looking like a "cud" of tobacco held in at the side of a chewer's mouth. Cuds may be found on the obverse, reverse or on the edge (collar die). Small cuds extending no further than the rim are referred to as "Rim Cuds."

Master Die — Die created from the master hub and used to produce working hubs.

Master Hub — A Hub used to produce master dies.

Mint Error – See Error.

Minting Process — The entire process leading up to and ending at the time the coin is struck. This includes: The designing of the coin, the production of master tools and dies, all phases of planchet production, and the actual striking of the coins.

Mint State (MS) – An uncirculated coin without wear; as struck. May be naturally toned by time or be brilliant.

Mintage — Number of coins struck for a given date and denomination or variety (when known).

Mint Mark Punch — A hand tool used for punching the Mint mark into a die.

Mint Mark — A letter punched into a die to indicate the Mint or origin. For example, the presence of a "P" below the date on a Roosevelt dime indicates it was struck by the Philadelphia Mint. Mint mark locations can and do often vary on the same denomination.

Multiple Variety (or multiple error) — A coin that features more than one type of die or minting variety or error.

National Collectors Association of Die Doubling (NCADD) — A club organized to study and share knowledge on die varieties.

COIN TERMS AND DEFINITIONS CONTINUED

Nicks or Bag marks — Contact marks in the form of abrasions, nicks and scratches on a coin caused by the coins falling upon each other (into tubs) during ejection from the presses and/or contact with each other while in shipping bags.

Numismatics — The study and collecting of coins, medals and tokens.

Obverse — The front or face side of the coin. Sometimes referred to as the "heads" side of the coin.

Off Metal Error — A coin that is struck on a planchet of the wrong composition than intended for a particular denomination. A cent struck on a dime planchet is an "off metal error." This category also includes U.S. coins struck on foreign planchets of the wrong alloy.

Over Mint Mark (OMM) – Refers to a coin that has two different Mint marks punched over one another. For example, the 1944-D/S cent with the D punched over an S is an OMM.

Oxidation — Tarnish or oxides on the surface on a coin from exposure to the environment.

Planchet — A blank that has had its rims raised via the upset mill and any other processing necessary to make it ready for striking. Often erroneously referred to as "Type-2 Blank" or the redundant "Type-2 Planchet."

Relief — Any design element that is raised above the field of the coin. Opposite of "incuse."

Repunched Mint Mark (RPM) – Any coin that shows multiple images of its Mint mark as a result of repunching. See the chapter on doubling.

Reverse — The back side of a coin. Also referred to as the "tails" side.

Rim Cud – These are much more common than major Cuds and normally do not constitute a premium. See Major Die Break.

Rim — A die break restricted to the rim area of the coin. The raised portion of the border between the coin field and outside edge of the coin.

Rotated Reverse — This occurs when the reverse and the obverse dies are not correctly aligned prior to the striking of coins. See the chapter on rotated reverses.

Scratch — Deep line or groove in the surface of a coin caused by contact with a sharp object.

Strike — The process of forming or stamping the design of a coin onto a planchet. Also refers to the strength or sharpness of the detail of the design impressed into the coin.

Toning (Tarnish) — Natural discoloration of a coin caused by exposure to the environment.

Tripled Die — The tripling of the features on a coin via the hubbing process. See Doubled Die Obverse or Doubled Die Reverse.

Uncirculated – A coin that has not circulated and shows no visible signs of wear. May be brilliant or toned.

Variety — Any coin that is recognizably different from another of the same design, date and type. Generally applied to variations that are considered "collectable."

Weak Strike — A weakness in the design features caused from too little pressure during striking. Often erroneously used to describe a coin struck from a worn die with mushy or weak details.

Working Die — A finished die used to produce coins versus a Master die used to create hubs.

Working Hub — A hub created from a master die, used to produce working dies.

FOREIGN COINS

A common question asked by newcomers to the hobby is what the values of foreign coins are. It is not uncommon to uncover foreign coins in circulating pocket change or in the small cigar box that a family member  set aside after vacation. While the value of foreign coinage can be difficult to determine without the proper references, for the most part the coins do not command large premiums and are generally worth sentimental value only. It is normally very difficult to sell foreign coins in small numbers but they may be sold by the pound to dealers at $8-$10 a pound — NOT each. The reference materials for foreign coins are often more expensive and difficult to read than the inscription on the coins. Current foreign coin pricing guides come in 1-3 volumes and can be priced at over $50 each. Use caution on foreign coins if you are out to make a fast dollar.

SELECTED VARIETIES

Jefferson Nickel struck on a planchet for a Lincoln Cent. The color of the coin will appear red or brown depending on the age and preservation of the coin. This is a highly desirable piece.

These are two different Roosevelt Dimes with a layer of clad missing. These type of coins will appear "Golden-brown" on one side. A coin with clad missing on both sides is extremely rare.

MISSING CLAD

Much like the Roosevelt Dime, the obverse of this Susan B Anthony Dollar is missing all the clad and will appear "Golden-Brown." The unaffected side will have a normal appearing color. Value: $350.00 - up.

PARTIAL UNPLATED

The arrows above point to the only remaining red color on this coin. The remainder of the coin appears a silver to silver gray.

Missing the Clad Layer
1999 Delaware States Quarter.

Obverse Value: $250.00 - up
Reverse Value: $450.00 - up

Missing the Clad Layer
1999 Georgia States Quarter.

Obverse Value: $250.00 - up
Reverse Value: $450.00 - up

Here is the much talked about Quarter obverse and Dollar reverse, "Mule." The entire coin will have the golden appearance of a 2000 Sacagawea Dollar. Value: $100,000.00

Brass Plated Lincoln Cents

Normal Appearance
Familiar Rosey Red

Brass Plating
Yellow-Brass Appearance

Value: $20 - $50

The Noncollectable "Mules"

A "mule" is a coin that is struck with a pair of dies not intended to be mated together. Undoubtedly the most famous "mule" known is the Washington quarter dollar obverse mated with the reverse of a Sacagawea dollar. Another famous rarity is the unique 1959 Lincoln cent with a "Wheat Ears" reverse – a reverse type that was discontinued in 1958! At least three different Roosevelt dime/Lincoln cent die pairings are known with the coins of each date or die combination being unique. Then there is the case of the two known examples of Washington quarter reverse dies paired together to create a two-tailed quarter!

All "mules" known on US coins are considered exceedingly rare with the most common being the Washington quarter/Sacagawea dollar "mule" with a total of only seven pieces known.

While we make note of these "mules," readers should be aware that most are unique and the chances of finding one are astronomically small (which is why we refer to them as noncollectables). Still, you never know, some of these pieces have reportedly been found by ordinary folks while going about their daily business — you could be the next person to find one!.

It needs to be pointed out that some specialists question the origins of some of these pieces. They ask how it is that with all of the safeguards in place, (that the Mint has claimed over the years would prevent such occurrences), that these coins could have escaped the Mint. At the time of this writing, the US Treasury Department is investigating the Washington quarter/Sacagawea dollar "mules" and is charging that some of them were removed from the Mint clandestinely while acknowledging that others left the Mint legitimately. The future legal status of some of these pieces is in question at this time.

Potential buyers or seller of such coins also need to know that "mules" are easily simulated by using two normal coins and machining one to fit into the other and gluing them together. Such concoctions are made in relatively large quantities and sold for a few dollars as novelty items. They often enter circulation after the buyers spend them by mistake. These may fool persons unaware of the diagnostics of the genuine error coins and be sold as errors by mistake.

As such, we recommend that anybody planning to buy or sell these coins check into their legal status and then have them certified by a professional grading/authentication service before entering into a transaction.

1959-D   "MULE" Wheat Reverse

Look at: The reverse of 1959-D Lincoln Cents.
Look for: A Wheat Reverse such as the reverses of 1909-1958.

VALUE:

Extra Fine	About Uncirculated	Uncirculated
		$48,300.00

Only one copy of this coin has ever been reported.

This is a very controversial coin, however it was reported to
be authentic by none other than the U.S. Mint. This coin is
easily counterfeited (see the "Two-Headed" article), **do not**
attempt to purchase this variety without the coin being authenticated by a professional.

PHOTO AND COIN COURTESY OF: Steve Bensen

1993-D 1c "MULE" Dime Reverse

Look at: The reverse of 1993-D Lincoln Cent.
Look for: A 1993-D Lincoln Cent with a Dime Reverse. This coin will have the same color and weight of a normal Lincoln Cent on both sides as it was struck on a cent blank.

VALUE:

Extra Fine	About Uncirculated	Uncirculated
		Estimate: $100,000 +

THIS COIN WAS DISCOVERED JUST PRIOR TO THE PUBLISHING. NO PHOTOS ARE AVAILABLE.

Only one copy of this coin has ever been reported.

Some specialists question if the origins of this variety, asking how it could have been produced and escaped the mint. However, it has been authenticated as genuine by the U.S. Treasury Department. Caution is in order if you plan on purchasing one of these because fakes are easily simulated. See the Chapter on the Two-Headed Coins and other mismatches.

Look at: A 1995 Lincoln Cent obverse and a dime reverse.
Look for: A dime reverse with a 1995-P Lincoln Cent Obverse. This coin will have the same color and weight of a normal Roosevelt dime.

VALUE:

Extra Fine   **About Uncirculated**   **Uncirculated**
Estimate: $125,000+

This coin could be worth up to $125.000.

Only one copy of this coin has ever been reported.

Some specialists question the origins of this variety, asking how it could have been produced and escaped the mint. However, it has been authenticated as genuine by the U.S. Treasury Department. Caution is in order if you plan on purchasing one of these because fakes are easily simulated. See the Chapter on the Two-Headed Coins and other mismatches.

PHOTO COURTESY OF: NGC, Numismatic Guarantee Corporation of America

1999-P 1c

Look at: The reverse of 1999-P Lincoln Cent.

Look for: A 1999-P Lincoln Cent with a Dime Reverse. This coin will have the same color and weight of a normal Lincoln Cent on both sides as it was struck on a cent blank.

VALUE:

Extra Fine	About Uncirculated	Uncirculated
	$125,000.00 - $250,000	

Only one copy of this coin has ever been reported.

Some specialists question the origins of this variety, asking how it could have been produced and escaped the mint. However, it has been authenticated as genuine by the U.S. Treasury Department. Caution is in order if you plan on purchasing one of these because fakes are easily simulated. See the Chapter on the Two-Headed Coins and other mismatches.

The photo shown above is a representation of the variety, not the actual "mule."

Look at: Quarters.

Look for: A Quarter with the reverse design on both the obverse and reverse.

VALUE:

Extra Fine	About Uncirculated	Uncirculated
		$70,000 - $80,000.00

PHOTO AND COIN COURTESY OF: Fred Weinberg

Look at: A 50 States Quarter obverse struck with a 2000 Sacagawea Reverse.
Look for: A golden colored coin with no date, a new states quarter front, and a back with the Sacagawea Eagle.

VALUE:

Extra Fine	About Uncirculated	Uncirculated
-	-	$30,000- $72,000

This is one of the greatest Mint errors of all time!!!!! The term "Mule" comes from an animal that is half donkey and half horse. This coin is neither but it is one-half quarter and one-half dollar. The Mint has acknowledged that this error occurred in an undetermined amount; there are currently three copies that we know of at the time of printing. The "Mule" error is the most valuable pocket change find; however, authentication by a professional service will be absolutely mandatory before offering the coin for sale. The coin shown here is authenticated and encapsulated by the Numismatic Guarantee Corporation of America.

PHOTO COURTESY OF: NGC, Numismatic Guarantee Corporation

2000-P "Mule" Sacagawea Dollar
Reverse w/ States Quarter Obverse

There are now ten (10) confirmed specimens of the Sacagawea Dollar/Quarter Mule. (December 3, 2001) The ten confirmed specimens are:

Mule #1. The "Discovery" specimen, found in Mountain Home, Arkansas. Originally sold by Bowers & Merena Auction Galleries at the 2000 ANA Philadelphia Millennium Sale for $29,900. Purchased in late June 2001 and then sold for $67,000. PCGS MS-66 (Die Pair #1)

Mule #2. The "eBay" specimen, sold by Delaware Valley Rare Coin Co., in Bromall Pennsylvania for $41,395 in July 2000. Purchased at the Heritage Numismatic Auctions Signature Sale held June 1, 2001 at the Long Beach Coin Expo for a then record price of $56,350. NGC MS-67 (Die Pair #2)

Mule #3. The "Heritage Auction" specimen, sold in the Heritage Numismatic Auction Pre-ANA Sale August 6, 2000 for $31,050. Currently in a private collection, after being purchased off an eBay Auction in October 2000. NGC MS-66 (Die Pair #2)

Mule #4. The "Margolis" specimen, originally from Fred Weinberg of Encino, CA. Sold by Arnold Margolis to a private collector in September 2000 for $47,500. PCGS MS-65 (Die Pair #1)

Mule #5. Found in Cape Girardeau, Missouri. This coin was discovered Sept. 2001 in change from a cashier at a cafeteria, and was in a 25-coin roll of Sacagawea $1, wrapped in a U.S. Mint designated paper wrapper. This piece is not on the market at this time. NGC MS-67 (Die Pair #3)

Mule #6. The "Fred Weinberg" specimen, discovered on the East Coast in June 2000 and sold by Fred Weinberg at the Long Beach Coin Expo October 5, 2000 for $50,000 to an anonymous collector. PCGS MS-66 (Die Pair #1)

Mule #7. The "Philadelphia" specimen, purchased from Maryland Coin Exchange in early February 2001 for $48,000. MCE purchased this piece from the man who discovered it in a roll of dollars in July 2000 in Pennsylvania. NGC MS-64 (Die Pair #2)

Mule #8. Purchased in June 2001. The purchase price was not disclosed. PCGS MS-66 (Die Pair #1)

Mule #9. This specimen purchased in July 2001. The purchase price was not disclosed. PCGS MS-65 (Die Pair #1)

Mule #10. The "Treasury" specimen, first reported in August 2001 by a convenience store owner who received it in payment in his downtown Philadelphia store in summer 2000. It was taken by Treasury Dept. officials in August 2001 to verify authenticity and to examine the piece at the Philadelphia Mint. It was returned by the Treasury Department in October 2001 and subsequently purchased by Fred Weinberg, who sold it in November 2001 for $70,000. NGC MS-65 (Die Pair #3)

ELEVENTH HOUR ADDITIONS

Just prior to publication several controversial varieties came in.

Not all experts agree on the exact nature of the variations and/or what they should be worth.

The authors of this book present them here for your pursuit without rending opinions on cause or worth but note that all are all currently selling at premium prices.

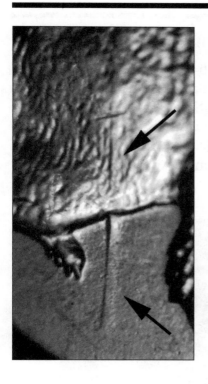

2005-D Buffalo 5c

This newly released Nickel sports an interesting "die dent" through the Buffalo's back and abdomen.

It is too early to estimate price and scarcity.

COIN COURTESY OF: Pamala Ryman   PHOTO COURTESY OF: Ken Potter

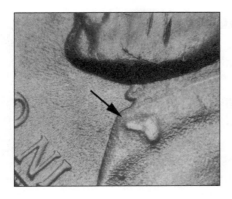

2004-D Jefferson Nickel

This die chip has been dubbed a "button-hole" variety because the location is Jefferson's collar.

This type of variety is not uncommon.

PHOTOS COURTESY OF: Billy G. Crawford

2004-D Roosevelt Dime

This 2004-D Roosevelt dime exhibits an anomaly just outside and through the ear. Some experts believe it is the result of a misaligned die clash, others a doubled die and still others feel it is a die gouge. Appears uncommon.

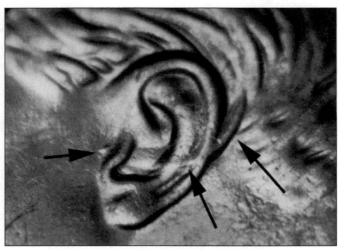

COIN COURTESY OF: Erik Nielson   PHOTO COURTESY OF: Ken Potter

2004-D Wisconsin 25c

Some believe the "extra" leaves (see arrows) are deliberate design modifications and others believe they are mere die gouges. Many thousands of each type are known.

Normal Appearance

"Low-Leaf" Variety

"High-Leaf" Variety

COIN COURTESY OF: Bill Fivaz   PHOTOS COURTESY OF: Ken Potter

2000-P Sacagawea "Golden" Dollar

This 2000 Sacagawea Reverse has a "die gouge protruding through the breast of the eagle.

This variety has been dubbed "Wounded Eagle."

"Wounded Eagle" Variety

COIN COURTESY OF: Gary Burger   PHOTO COURTESY OF: Ken Potter

BIBLIOGRAPHY

Anderson, Shane M. *The Complete Lincoln Cent Encyclopedia*, Krause Publications, Iola, WI, 1996.

ANACS, Population Report, 11/1998.

Breen, Walter. Walter *Breen's Complete Encyclopedia of U.S. And Colonial Coins*. New York, NY: Doubleday, 1988.

Errorscope. Seattle: CONECA. James Wiles. Volume 6 Number 6, pages 8-9, James Wiles.

Fivaz, Bill and J.T. Stanton. *The Cherrypickers' Guide to Rare Die Varieties*, 3rd edition. Wolfeboro, NH: Powers and Merena Galleries, Inc., 1984.

Margolis, Arnold. *The Error Coin Encyclopedia*, 2nd edition, 1994.

Noe, Geoffrey, Silver Dollar Company Inc., *The Illustrated Error Coin Pricing Guide*, Woodhaven, NY 09/10/91.

Numismatic News, Iola WI: Krause Publications. September 15, 1998.

Potter, Ken. Doubling Worthless Or Valuable? Lathrup Village, Michigan. 1994.

Romines, Delma. The One Cent Doubled Die Update, Del Romines, 1990.

Rotated Die Coin Census, 1999.

Teletrade Inc. Real Time Price Guide, 1996/1997.

Wagnon, Gary., Karen Peterson and Kevin Flynn. *A Quick Reference to the Top Lincoln Cent Die Varieties*, Rancocas, NJ, Archive Press Inc,1998.

Wexler, John; Bill Crawford and Kevin Flynn. *The Authoritative Reference to Eisenhower Dollars*, Archive Press, NJ, 1998.

Wexler, John and Kevin Flynn. *The Authoritative Reference to Lincoln Cents*, KCK Press, NJ, 1996.

Wexler, John and Ed Miller. *The RPM Book*, 1983.

Wiles, James. *The RPM Book*, 2nd edition - Lincoln Cents, Savannah, GA, Stanton Printing and Publishing, 1997.

FINAL TIPS

1. Look at as many possible coins as you can. The more you examine, the greater your odds of uncovering your fortune.

2. Be patient, if you don't find anything immediately, keep looking.

3. Don't expect to sell everything you find immediately – wait for the proper time and place to maximize your profits.

4. When available, use the Internet! There are many great auction venues for selling your coins, buying books, supplies, and making contacts.

5. Many of the smaller errors do not sell quickly, particularly in circulated condition. You may want to stock them up for a bulk sale.

6. Do not expect to sell your find immediately. It may take some effort on your part. Purchase a coin magazine, use the Internet, contact a local dealer or even write letters. Coins are no different than any other business. You will have to market your product to be successful.

7. Buy a few other books to widen your search. Even if you do not collect coins, the hunt and treasure are worth the effort.

8. Separate particular dates of a denomination until you have several of a particular year. This will assist you with years that have numerous varieties.

9. DO NOT only look for the errors listed in the book; there are thousands of other varieties that are already known and many more others unreported.

10. Try looking in new Bank Wrapped rolls from your bank. These rolls contain most of the errors that are found in circulation. Get them early.

11. Not unlike anything else, you may take a bump or two in the process of trying to sell a coin. Not all will sell quickly, and you will not get the listed price. If you are serious about making money, you must research and market your product.

Perseverance is the key to Striking It Rich With Pocket Change.

Ken Potter is 54 years old and began collecting coins in 1959 when the reverse of the Lincoln cent was changed from the wheat-back to the now familiar Lincoln Memorial design. He dabbled in varieties and errors almost from the very beginning of his collecting career and began specializing in that area in 1979 when he discovered a new variety on a Canadian dollar that made front page news in the Canadian numismatic press.

He's a member in good standing in the *Numismatic Literary Guild (NLG)* and a charter life member of the *Combined Organizations of Numismatic Error Collectors of America (CONECA)*. He's served on *CONECA's* Board of Directors in the past and currently serves on its Board overseeing the club's public relations program. He's *CONECA's* Michigan State Representative and *CONECA's* longest serving doubled die attributer (unofficially since 1981 and officially since 1985). He's currently the official attributer of world doubled dies for both *CONECA* and the newly formed *National Collectors Association of Die Doubling (NCADD)*. He privately lists doubled dies and all other variety types on both U.S. and other world coins in the *Variety Coin Register®*. He's a member of the Board of Directors of the *Lincoln Cent Society (LCS)* and a frequent contributor to it's newsletter, the *Centinel.*

He is a prolific author and photographer with regularly featured columns in the following publications: *Coin World's - Varieties Notebook, World Coin News' - Visiting Varieties, Canadian Coin News' - "Varieties", Cherrypickers' News' - Cherrypickin' the World, Cherrypickers' News' - Mintmark Madness, The NCADD Hub's - Die Doubling World, The Michigan State Numismatic Society (MSNS) Mich-Matist's - Michigan Cherries, The CONECA ErrorScope's - World Goodies from the Variety Coin Register and The LCS Centinel's, Varieties & Errors* column.

He's a member of the American Numismatic Association, NLG, MSNS-LM, CONECA-LM, NCADD-FM, Northwest Detroit Coin Club, LCS, Birmingham-Bloomfield Coin Club, COINMASTERS, Worldwide Bimetallic Coin Club and Riverside Coin Club.

He's been employed with DaimlerChrysler for 32 years and has operated a mail order business since 1973. Other interests include, fishing, the outdoors, music, computers and spending time with his 19 year old daughter, Anna.

Brian Allen is 37 years old and began collecting coins in 1989 after his father gave him a small bag of Wheat Cents. Brian dedicates most of his collecting efforts at searing for error and varieties in circulating pocket change.

He has made numerous variety coin discoveries; He has had numerous articles published in the National Collectors Association of Die Doubling bi-monthly newsletter *the HUB*, and has co-authored two additional books, *The Complete Price Guide and Cross-Reference to Lincoln Cent Mint Mark Varieties* and *The Comprehensive Guide to Lincoln Cent RPMs-Volume 1*.

He's the former Public Relations Director and a Founding Member of the *National Collector's Association of Die Doubling (NCADD)*, a member of the *Combined Organization of Numismatic Error Collectors of America (CONECA)*, *The American Numismatic Association*, *Numismatic Literary Guild*, and the *Cape Fear Coin Club* in Fayetteville, NC. Currently, Brian is the official attributer of US Gold, Fifty-Cent and One-Dollar Doubled Dies for *The National Collectors association of Die Doubling (NCADD)*.

He is a native of Clayton, Illinois and served in the US Army from 1990 to 2005. During his 15 years of Active Duty he graduated numerous elite military course that include; Special Forces Medical Sergeants Course, US Army Ranger Course, French Language Course, Military Free-Fall, Jumpmaster, Airborne, Pathfinder, and possess numerous other military qualifications. Brian is a Nationally Registered Emergency Medical Technician-Paramedic and still currently serves in the Drilling Inactive Reserve, as a US Army Special Forces Medic. Brian served in Operation Desert Shield/Storm (1990-1991) and Operation Enduring Freedom (Afghanistan 2002) where he was awarded the Bronze Star Medal for Valor.

He earned a Bachelor's Degree in Health Science from Campbell University, Buies Creek, North Carolina in 2000 and is currently an Osteopathic Medical Student at Pikesville College School of Osteopathic Medicine (PCSOM), Pikeville, KY.

In addition to coin collecting, Brian enjoys running, basketball, baseball, fishing and weight-lifting. Brian is the son of Betty and Dale Allen of Clayton, Illinois and the father of Hannah and Jacob Allen. He currently resides in Pikeville, KY.

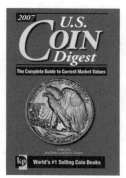